65p
13/-

Published in Great Britain by
World Distributors (Manchester) Limited,
P.O. Box 111, 12 Lever Street, Manchester M60 1TS

Printed and bound in England by
Jarrold and Sons Limited, Norwich

SBN 7235 0119 X

CONTENTS

MEET THE DOUBLE DECKERS

Climb aboard the double decker bus and come and meet:

SCOOPER
Scooper is the natural leader of the Double Deckers. He combines a love of adventure and a ready wit with plenty of common-sense. He makes sure that none of the Double Deckers' jokes get really out-of-hand, and can laugh just as readily when the joke's on him as if he had played it on someone else. His joint seconds-in-command are:

SPRING, who loves to fool about, especially on the stage in a clever song-and-dance act, which usually includes some brilliant impressions of famous people in show business, zany humour and slapstick comedy and

BRAINS peers at the world through his owl-like spectacles, and for someone who prides himself on his scientific turn of mind he comes up with some very wild ideas, and the results of some of his experiments in his lab in the den have to be seen to be believed!

DOUGHNUT is an extremely plump, good-natured fellow, whose idea of bliss is a bagful of doughnuts followed by another bagful of doughnuts—hence his nickname! Although placid, Doughnut is never lost for a witty retort and can liven up quickly should he be asked to take part in a show. He doesn't even mind a custard pie in his face—after all, some of it goes in his mouth!

BILLIE likes nothing better than to escape into a world of fantasy where she becomes the leading lady in a hit musical, or has a record in the Top Ten! But in her more realistic moments she is a great little tomboy, daring any of the boys to say that they can do something that she can't, and calming them down if the argument gets too heated!

STICKS, whose great love is music, especially the kind he plays himself on the drums whenever the Double Deckers put on one of their many shows to show off their versatile talent. But he also has a roguish sense of humour, as all the Double Deckers can ruefully testify.

TIGER is the youngest Double Decker and regarded with great affection by the rest, who are always careful to include her in all the gang's activities. They tease her occasionally about being inseparable from her pet tiger mascot—but not too much, because when young Tiger is angry she uses her mascot as a weapon, and even toy tigers can hurt when they are used as battering rams!

BRAINS' BRAINWAVE

"Thank heaven's he's stopped tinkering with the engine at last," cried Billie, as silence reigned in the den for the first time for several days. "Brains must have given up at last. I told him it would be impossible to get the bus working. All the works are rusted from standing about so long. I knew it was an impossible task he had set himself . . . but you know Brains, he just won't give up."

"Nothing is impossible, Billie, given time, patience, and the necessary know-how," interrupted Brains, walking in just at that moment. "And you are quite wrong about the reason I've stopped work. I haven't given up at all, merely got the engine working at last."

He threw out this last remark with studied casualness, but the reaction from the other Double Deckers was all that Brains had secretly hoped it would be.

"Well, that will be easily arranged," said Sticks, airily. "There's a good film down at the Roxy, and I've got enough of my birthday money left to pay for all our seats."

"What are we waiting for then?" cried Doughnut, cramming the last piece of a large bar of chocolate into his mouth. "Come along, everyone, we can buy some popcorn to eat inside."

"You're always thinking about something to eat," laughed Scooper, as he gave Doughnut a good-natured push in the direction of the door.

He shepherded the rest of them towards the door as Brains took the necessary steps to open it. But, as he himself turned to go, he said curiously: "What are you up to, Brains? We don't want to come back and find the den in ruins. I can remember some of your chemistry experiments of old."

"Don't worry, Scooper. What I am trying to do will perhaps make us all a fortune," replied Brains seriously.

Scooper was about to pursue the matter further, but the others were calling impatiently to him to hurry up. He sighed and said, "Well, remember what I said, Brains," as off he went.

"Gosh, Brains, that's terrific!" cried Scooper. "Does that mean we will be able to drive it round the yard?"

"Or to the zoo or the seaside?" shouted Tiger, giving full rein to her imagination.

But Spring's quick eyes had noticed Brains' somewhat doubtful expression as the others threw questions at him. "Is there some small problem, as usual, Brains?" he chuckled. "Such as lack of petrol?" he cried, getting sudden inspiration. "Ah, I see that there is. Well, sorry, old man, but it's no use expecting help from me. I'm stoney broke at the moment."

"Why pick on this moment?" retorted Brains, rather sarcastically. "You are always broke. Anyway, you need not worry. I am not asking any of you for money. All I want is to be left in peace here in the den for the rest of the afternoon."

Brains watched them until they reached the gates and then, with a sigh of relief, he returned to his lab where a strange, green-coloured liquid was bubbling away merrily in a retort.

He consulted a very dusty-looking book, which was lying on the lab bench, and smiled to himself. "It was a spot of luck finding this old book in the junk market down the street," he murmured aloud. "Fancy nobody spotting the fact that it is full of old recipes, especially the one which shows how to make petrol from such everyday ingredients as seaweed and cooking fat."

He set about finding a number of containers for the liquid, which was sending off a rather strange smell, and which changed to various shades of green every few seconds.

After filling several old petrol cans there was still a little of the liquid over, so Brains poured it into an old shoe tin, a shampoo bottle and an old Coke tin.

"Waste not, want not," he murmured with a grin. "I think I'll just nip down to the Roxy until the petrol cools down a bit. The big picture might not have started yet."

And, luckily for Brains, the picture hadn't started. But in the darkness he could not find his friends, and he was forced to sit alone.

This seemingly unimportant force of circumstance had disastrous consequences back at the den, where some of the Double Deckers knew nothing about the newly-made petrol.

Tiger and Billie had left the cinema early when they discovered the film was a Western, and Billie decided to fill in the time until the others arrived back by washing her hair.

She was delighted to find a bottle of green shampoo which gave a lovely lather. Returning to Tiger with a towel swathed around her head, she found the youngest Double Decker gazing in horror at a dark green stain on her new red leather boots.

"Oh, Billie, just look at my boots," she wailed. "I decided to polish them with this leather cleaner in this tin, but this terrible stain appeared, and although I have rubbed and rubbed I still can't get it out."

"Here, let me try," comforted Billie, pulling the towel from her head at the same time, intending to use it as a duster. "Tiger, whatever is the matter?" she asked in astonishment, as a look of horror crossed her little friend's face and her mouth fell open with astonishment.

"Your hair . . . your hair . . . it's turned *green*," gasped Tiger, pointing a shaking finger at Billie's head.

"Green . . . nonsense . . . you need your eyes testing," began Billie. But as Tiger's expression remained the same, she seized a hand-mirror and gazed at herself. "Oh, you're right, it must be that shampoo I used," she wailed. "I'll go and wash my hair again. Perhaps the colour will come out then."

"I'll come with you to give it a good rinse," said Tiger, trying to help. "And I'll use some soap and water on my boots while I'm about it."

The two girls disappeared just as Sticks and Scooper arrived back followed a moment later by Doughnut, carrying a Coke tin.

"Look, I've just found an opened, fizzy drink," he said, waving it about in the air. "It smells rather peculiar, but it will help to quench my thirst. Those salted peanuts have made me very thirsty."

"Wait a moment, Doughnut, let me look at that tin," cried Billie, her green hair floating round her shoulders as she rushed into the room.

But Billie's warning came too late for, as Doughnut drank thirstily, before their astonished eyes his face changed to exactly the same shade of green as Billie's hair and Tiger's boots.

"Just wait till I see Brains," shouted Billie.

"This really is the limit. We can't go around with green hair and faces, and it's a shame about poor Tiger's new boots."

"Really, Billie, I'm sure that you are worrying unnecessarily," said Brains, who chose just that moment to walk into the den. "And actually, it *is* rather your own fault for using something that didn't belong to you!"

"Well, I like that!" said Billie indignantly. "That's a charming sentiment, I must say."

"Look, Billie, perhaps Brains is right," cried Tiger suddenly. "The stain on my boot has almost disappeared, and I am sure that your hair is not quite as green as it was before."

"But my face is still as green as grass," wailed Doughnut.

"Give it time. I'm sure it will wear off soon," replied Brains confidently, as he filled the petrol tank to the brim with the green liquid. He lifted up the bonnet and then started up the engine.

For a moment there was silence, and then the engine sprang to life with a mighty roar.

"Look, everyone, it's really working," cried Brains in delight.

The others gathered round, amazed to see all the machinery working smoothly at last. And then, suddenly, before their astonished eyes, all the metal turned slowly bright green in colour, and then disintegrated into a pile of rusty, green, scrap metal.

"Well, that's that. Now we know we can never get it on the road," announced Scooper firmly. "And I absolutely forbid you to try out any more experiments in our den until I give you permission, Brains. Although all the green has completely disappeared from Billie's hair, and Doughnut's face seems to be getting back to normal, this experiment could have had serious consequences."

At any other time Brains would have been prepared to argue loud and long about Scooper's decision, but now he was so depressed about the failure of his experiment, which meant the end to all his secret hopes, that he merely nodded his head sadly.

Now that everything had returned to normal, the other Double Deckers began to feel rather sorry for Brains, because they knew that he longed to be able to drive a double decker bus through real streets.

"Cheer up, Brains," said little Tiger, giving his arm a squeeze. "I can quite see the funny side, now that my boots are as good as new. And, come to think of it, Billie looked very pretty with her green hair."

"Pretty queer," replied Billie, with a rueful grin. "Still, no harm was done in the long run, so I forgive you, Brains. I suppose we must all be prepared to make sacrifices in the interests of science."

"Hark at her," said Spring, rather rudely. "Oh, look, there's Albert, and he looks very excited. I wonder what's up!"

"Let's go and see," suggested Billie, thinking it was time the subject of the experiment was dropped. "Hello, Albert, have you come up on the pools?"

"No such luck!" replied Albert, their favourite grown-up friend. "But us dustbin men have been chosen to lead the Spirit of London carnival."

"Well done," cried Scooper, clapping Albert on the back. "What is your float going to look like?"

"A double decker bus," grinned Albert. "And I've come to ask if you lot would like to be passengers aboard the bus. In fact," he added, with a sly glance in the direction of Brains, "one of you could be in the driving seat of the bus, if you like."

"Do you mean it, Albert?" cried Brains, seeing a way for his dream to come true at last.

"Sure," replied Albert, beaming from ear to ear. "Of course, the float would be on a lorry, but the bus will be a replica of a real bus, down to its controls and engine. So it would seem as if you were really driving it."

"Will the bus have an open top?" asked Spring eagerly. "If it does, we could put on a show for the spectators, couldn't we? They like to be entertained, as they stand watching on the pavements. It helps them to forget how hard those pavements are."

Everyone laughed at this, but Sticks added quickly: "I think that is a splendid idea, Spring. We could put on a minstrel show, and I could play my drums."

"And we could sing and tell jokes," the others added eagerly, not to be outdone.

"You'd all better start practising then," warned Albert. "The carnival's on Saturday, regardless of the state of the weather."

But, fortunately, the weatherman was kind, producing a cloudless blue sky for the carnival.

Charity collectors rattled their boxes all along the route, and the Double Deckers were delighted when Tiger and her pet mascot had the heaviest box at the end of the day. The others sang and joked their way to success as their float headed the parade, while Brains sat proudly at the controls of the bus, happy that his long-held ambition had been realised at last.

Climb on Board

Double-decker buses are, of course, a very common sight in England, but in other lands they would present a very unusual way of travelling indeed. Each country has transport which has been adapted to suit its needs, and very often the cost comes into it too, as in the case of . . .

Coconut Rafts

These rafts are made of coconuts, believe it or not. The natives of the Philippine Islands gently float down river to market on such rafts. On arrival, the rafts are carefully dismantled and the coconuts sold! Not only an ideal way of travelling, but a very profitable one, too!

Gondolas

The Venetians also are very fond of travelling by water. The narrow Italian waterways in Venice are a scene of constant hurrying to and fro as the gaily coloured gondolas float along, carrying passengers, newlyweds and even the sick. Yes, they have police gondolas, ambulance gondolas, taxi gondolas, and even large gondolas instead of buses. But they haven't got double-decker ones—not yet, anyway.

Kufas

These strange tub-shaped boats are to be found on the River Tigris in Iraq. The natives make them out of the reeds that grow by the sides of the river and the skins from the animals which they catch. The craft is pushed along with a long pole, but I don't think that it would be much like punting on a calm English river on a Sunday afternoon.

Boats of Woven Reeds

Such fragile-looking boats as these are to be seen on a very famous lake in South America: Lake Titicaca, which is on the border between Peru and Bolivia. The boats are made completely out of rushes, even the sails, which look very much like rush matting.

Rickshaws

Back on land again, this time in China, where gay rickshaws are drawn through the streets, although mostly for tourists nowadays. The rickshaws carry only one passenger as a rule, and are pulled not by an animal, but by a Chinaman!

In the country districts of China, farmers often use strange wheelbarrows for transport, especially if they have a lot to carry, or a family to move.

Sledges in Madeira

These are also used mainly for the tourists, but this time on the sunshine island of Madeira, where they still have a lot of cobbled streets. Instead of having transport with wheels they have gay sledges, like this one, which glide quite smoothly over the bumpy cobbles. And, as you can see, they also have nice canopies to protect their passengers from the sun. The sledges are usually pulled along by strong oxen.

Travois

This kind of transport dates back hundreds of years, right back to the famous Indians of Wild West fame, and even before that. The Indians that remain in North America still use these Travois, whenever they have a lot to carry, or when the family has to move to another camp.

Monorail

This is a monorail railway carriage, which can run on one rail, instead of two, unlike ordinary trains. Monorail trains can travel very quickly and with less noise than ordinary trains. Germany has one and so does America, and in Japan they have a monorail which links the city of Tokyo to the airport; it is $8\frac{1}{2}$ miles long.

TRICKED again!

Spring loves playing tricks on people, especially on the other Double Deckers; in fact, you could say that it's his hobby. Here are some of the ones that he's been practising recently; you might like to try them out yourself.

Come on, Let's Move

All that Spring uses for this trick is a small sheet of glass, two thick books and some tissue paper.

He cuts out some figures about ½" high from the tissue paper. He usually uses the Double Deckers as models.

When finished, the figures are carefully placed under the sheet of glass, which is placed on top of the two thick books, as shown.

All that is necessary now is to rub the glass quickly with a handkerchief or soft cloth, and the figures will immediately begin to move about, as if they are dancing.

He's a Real Card!

Tiger falls for this card trick every time. Spring asks her to stand opposite him, about two feet away, and then takes out his pack of cards. As Tiger watches him very closely, he turns the top card only face upwards, and turns the pack round to show Tiger the card. Of course, he can then see the bottom card, which he memorises.

Tiger isn't very impressed when Spring tells her the suit and number of the card which he has just turned up and shown her, because she knows that Spring has already seen it. But when he puts the cards behind his back and quickly places the card that he had memorised, face upwards, to show Tiger, she is very impressed indeed, because she doesn't know that Spring has already seen it. In fact he can go right through the pack doing this, because each time that he shows Tiger the top card, he can see the bottom one, which will be moved to the top behind his back. Clever, isn't it?

Magic Match

This trick is very simple too, when you know how to do it! Spring gives each of the Double Deckers a match, which they have to try to stand up on end on a smooth surface. Try as they might, they always fail, but Spring doesn't. The match that he keeps for himself has had its wooden end dipped in a drop of water, and this is all that is needed to make the match stand on end and stay there. Try it; just wet the end and then place firmly on a smooth surface and success will be yours, too.

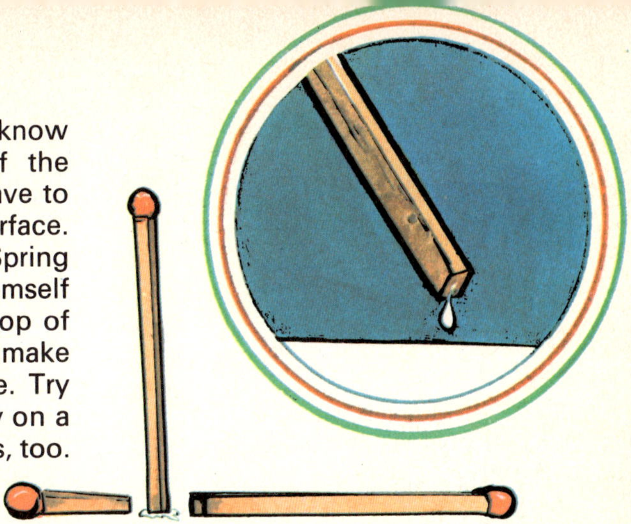

Brains also likes to try out tricks on his friends, but his are usually of a more scientific nature, like the ones that he's allowed us to show you here.

Hey Presto!

You've probably all seen that trick where the magician pulls out a tablecloth from underneath a table full of crockery. But this is a trifle difficult for beginners and your mother might not be so pleased if it doesn't succeed first time. So why not try it Brains' way? There's less likely to be a disaster this way!

All that you need for this trick is a glass, a thin piece of card and a penny. Simply place the card on top of the glass and the penny on top of that. Now, using your thumb and middle finger, flick the card away from underneath the penny, which will then fall into the glass. The reason why the penny does not get carried away with the card is the speed at which the card is flicked away, leaving the inert object—in this case the penny—still in the same place.

The Rising Egg

This trick requires a hard-boiled egg and three tumblers. Into tumbler A put about four inches of water and the hard-boiled egg, into tumbler B some more water, and into tumbler C some water to which salt has been added.

Now, ask someone to pour more water from tumbler B into tumbler A, in an attempt to make the egg rise from the bottom of the glass. Nothing will happen. Now it's your turn. Pour all the water out of tumbler A and pour in the water which you've got in tumbler C. Amazingly, the egg will begin to rise. Just listen to your friends gasp with surprise.

The answer is a simple one, the density of salt water is greater. So the egg floats, in just the same way that you find it easier to float in sea-water, which is salty, than in ordinary water.

Scooper's Sponsored Walk

"I wonder what Scooper wants us all for so urgently?" said Billie to Tiger, as the two girls joined the rest of the Double Deckers in their den, early one Saturday morning. "He doesn't usually send us a letter by post. It must be something important."

"It is," said Scooper, who had just overheard Billie's last words. "You see, I wanted to make sure that I spoke to you all before you had a chance to spend all your pocket money for the week. I've agreed to walk in the charity walk to raise money for parcels for old people for Christmas, and I want you all to sponsor me, at threepence a mile."

"What a good idea! Of course we will!" burst out Tiger immediately.

The others nodded their heads in agreement, but Doughnut said doubtfully: "How many miles do you intend to walk, Scooper, and how will we know that you finish the course?"

"The walk lasts for ten miles," explained Scooper patiently, "from the top of the High Street up to the crossroads just by the farm. And there are check points every mile, Doughnut, where I will have my card marked to show I have passed by."

"That will be two shillings and sixpence, if you finish," said Doughnut, doing a rapid sum.

"Cheer up, Doughnut, that will still leave you some money for your usual feast of cakes and ice cream," chuckled Sticks. "I say, everybody, I've just had a wonderful idea. Let's all go on the walk to keep Scooper company."

"More like to keep an eye on me so that I won't be tempted to hitch a lift," laughed Scooper. "But come along if you like, the more the merrier!"

So, exactly an hour later, after making sure that Scooper had his walk scorecard safely stowed away in his pocket, the Double Deckers set off gaily.

"You know, this is quite pleasant," said Doughnut, as he and Spring walked along together. "Especially now that we have left the town behind and have come into the country."

"Let's hope you feel as happy at the end of the walk," chuckled Scooper, who was leading the group. "We have to climb over this stile now, everybody. Can you manage all right, young Tiger?"

"Manage . . . you're speaking to the leading member of the junior gymnastic team," retorted Tiger, climbing the stile nimbly. "Oh dear, look at poor old Doughnut; he's stuck!"

"You carry on, Scooper, we'll rescue old fatty," cried Spring and Sticks. "We'll push from behind, Billie, and you pull him over in front."

"Hey, steady on, I'm made of flesh and blood, you know," moaned Doughnut, as he was pulled and pushed in every direction.

"More flesh than blood, I think," cried Sticks, as with a mighty thud Doughnut was pushed over the stile and landed on the ground. "Oh, lor', run everyone, here comes a bull! Scooper might have warned us that there was one in this field which we have to cross."

"And Spring's wearing a bright red shirt," groaned Billie. "Run quickly, Spring, before the bull spots you."

But Bertie the bull had already seen the blaze of red and, ignoring the rest of the Double Deckers, he made straight for poor Spring. Although Spring was an extremely swift runner the bull was even faster and, before he could reach the opposite gate, the bull had tossed

him over the gate and he landed slap into the middle of a bed of very prickly nettles.

The bull then appeared to lose all interest and wandered over to a clump of cow parsley, while the rest of the Double Deckers crowded round Spring.

"Are you hurt, Spring?" asked Billie sympathetically. "Look, there's a rustic seat over there. Let's rest awhile before we go on."

"I don't think I'll be able to sit down again for at least a week," groaned Spring, as he gingerly started to remove some nettles from the seat of his trousers. "Scooper should have told us this was a dangerous walk and I would have come prepared, in my bullet-proof suit."

"You look hot, Spring," cried Tiger, attempting to help. "There's a stream over there. Let's all have a drink there. The water looks beautifully clean and cool."

"Watch out for the crocodiles, Tiger," teased Sticks as the youngest Double Decker rushed towards the stepping stones over the stream.

"A tiger can always fight off a crocodile," she replied airily, as she took her first step onto the stones. But, quite suddenly, a large fish popped its head out of the water and, taken unawares, Tiger gave a little scream of alarm. She wobbled on the stones and, unable to retain her balance, fell with a great splash into the water, as the poor fish swam away in alarm.

"Now you've frightened away the poor little fish," mocked Sticks.

Then, seeing how wet and bedraggled and frightened Tiger looked, Sticks took off his own shoes and socks and waded in and rescued her.

"Don't worry, Tiger, your clothes will soon dry out in the sun," comforted Billie. "I will wait for you, it will give me a chance to rest my feet. I was an idiot not to wear proper walking shoes for this expedition. Already I've got a really big blister on one of my heels, and it is very painful."

"Scooper would grumble at us all if he could see us now," smiled Sticks. "He thinks we can't look after ourselves without his help."

"Now, no quarrelling!" ordered Billie, taking command of the situation. "I think that is a good idea, Brains. Will you climb the tree?" she finished innocently, with a wicked twinkle in her eye, for she knew that Brains hated physical exercise almost as much as Doughnut did.

"No, I'll leave it to Sticks, he's as agile as a monkey, as well as having some of that animal's more obvious traits," retorted Brains, skilfully avoiding the playful blow that Sticks aimed at him.

"Right you are," replied Sticks, and he swiftly climbed up the tallest tree that he could find, as the others gathered around it on the ground.

"What can you see, Sticks?" asked Tiger eagerly. "Can you see Scooper?"

"Yes, way out in the distance," Sticks called down. "And it seems to be his day for helping people. He's just pumped up a flat tyre for a cyclist, and now he's joined a group of people trying to get a man's car out of a ditch. Oh, well done, they've managed it, and Scooper's on his way again. Come along, let's see if we can catch him up."

"Won't stopping to help people penalise Scooper in the race?" asked tender-hearted Tiger, thinking of the food parcels for the old people.

"Oh, no, in this race all you need to do is finish. The time you take does not matter at all," Billie assured her quickly. Suddenly there was a tearing sound, and she added, "Oh dear, Sticks, you've torn your jacket on that branch as you came down. What a pity!"

"And he *could* be right," admitted Billie with a rueful shake of her head. "He has only been gone a few minutes and look what's happened already! Spring is chased by a bull, Tiger falls in the stream, and I have a blister, to say nothing of Doughnut getting stuck in a stile."

"And do you realise," put in Spring suddenly, "that only Scooper has a copy of the route? As he appears to be nowhere in sight, I must therefore presume that we are lost."

"Very clever, Sherlock Holmes," cried Brains, who up to that moment had kept remarkably silent. "But we are not lost at all. All we need is for someone to climb one of those trees over there and spy out the land. We are sure to see Scooper, or one of the other competitors, in the distance."

"Aye, aye, Long John, have you got your telescope with you?" retorted Sticks, with heavy sarcasm.

"It was only an old one, don't worry," Sticks assured her. "It seems to be a walk full of accidents. Only clever old Brains has kept intact so far."

"Don't tempt fate," warned Billie and, as if to prove her words Brains suddenly tripped over a root and fell heavily to the ground.

"Brains, old son, are you all right?" asked Sticks, feeling very guilty as he rushed over to the bespectacled Double Decker. "I wasn't wishing you any harm, I swear it."

"Of course not, it was my own clumsy fault," replied Brains, looking very white as he tried to stand on his feet. A small cry of pain made him sit down again hurriedly, and as Billie gently drew off his shoe they could all see that Brains' foot was badly swollen.

"Here, Spring, go and dip this in the stream," ordered Billie, "and I will put a cold compress on his ankle until we get home."

Spring took the clean handkerchief which Billie held out to him. He ran quickly over to the stream and dipped it in the cool water.

"Gee, thanks, Billie, that feels better already," said Brains gratefully, as Billie quickly bound it skilfully around his injured ankle.

"Just call me Florence Nightingale," laughed Billie, secretly very relieved to see the colour returning to Brains' cheeks. "But you mustn't walk on your ankle again for a bit, Brains. You will have to rest it for a few days."

"But how will we get him home?" cried Tiger. "It's too far for the boys to carry him, isn't it?"

"If we could just get him to the final check-

point, the organisers have laid on a fleet of cars to get the competitors home," said Spring. "Scooper told me this morning before we set off. I'm sure that, in the circumstances, one of the drivers will give Brains a lift home."

"But we will have to get him to the checkpoint first," worried Billie. "Look, there's a hay waggon over there going in the right direction. Run over and explain, Sticks. Perhaps he will take us."

The friendly driver was most sympathetic and very willing to help in any way he could. He easily lifted Brains onto the waggon in his strong arms, and although Brains was rather embarrassed at being carried, he was very pleased to sink down among the soft hay and so ease the pain in his foot.

The other Double Deckers laughed and joked with Giles the driver, and in no time at all they had arrived at the checkpoint, just as Scooper was having his final time marked on his card.

"I did it, everyone!" he called, waving his completed card triumphantly in the air. "That's two shillings and sixpence you all owe me."

Everyone gladly dug in their pockets for the money, except Doughnut, who said doubtfully: "How do we know that you walked ten miles?"

The others rounded on him indignantly, but Scooper merely rolled up his trouser leg with a huge grin. "I thought *you* might prove awkward, Doughnut, my boy," he chuckled. "So I strapped a pedometer to my leg, which records the mileage I walked. Look, ten miles exactly from the first to the last checkpoint. Now are you satisfied? Come on, pay up and look cheerful about it. After all, it's for a good cause!"

Scooper grinned from ear to ear as the coins rattled in his charity tin, and the other Double Deckers were very proud of him when they discovered that he was the first to complete the course.

Later, as they were all driven home in a car, Billie said: "Well, it certainly was a walk full of mishaps, but it was well worth it." And, thinking of the pleasure the Christmas parcels would give, the rest of the Double Deckers heartily agreed!

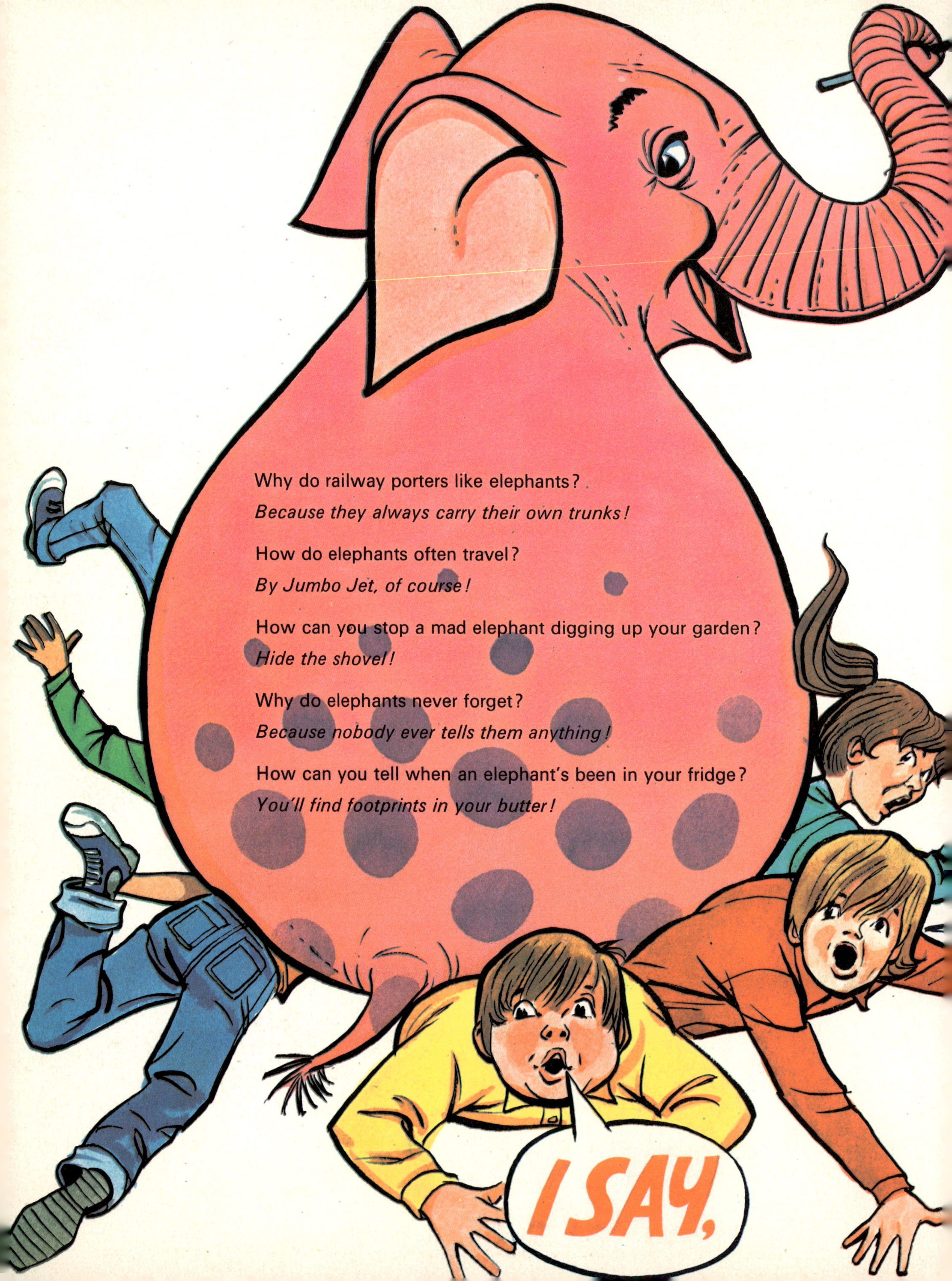

Why do railway porters like elephants?

Because they always carry their own trunks!

How do elephants often travel?

By Jumbo Jet, of course!

How can you stop a mad elephant digging up your garden?

Hide the shovel!

Why do elephants never forget?

Because nobody ever tells them anything!

How can you tell when an elephant's been in your fridge?

You'll find footprints in your butter!

HAVING TO WORK UP HERE REMINDS ME OF THE JOKE ABOUT THE PAINTER WHO STEPPED BACK TO ADMIRE HIS WORK!
OH, GERALD, YOU'VE RUINED YOUR NEW HAT!
IT'S QUITE SIMPLE. IF YOU DON'T LIKE MY WORK THEN WHY DON'T YOU FIRE ME?
I SAY...
I SAY,
THIS IS GOING TO HURT ME FAR MORE THAN IT IS YOU.
WELL, GIVE ME SIX OF THE BEST THEN!
OH! THAT'S WHERE MY KNITTING WENT TO!

Doughnut's Gourmands' Club

Doughnut, that greedy gourmand, is eager to start a club for foodlovers like himself, but he is having difficulty in finding enough members, as he insists that they answer all these questions before qualifying for membership. Are you bright enough to join this very exclusive club and gain a Golden Doughnut Club badge?

1. What is another name for 'golden hands'? Bananas
2. Complete the following by adding a nationality:
   a) French beans
   b) Hungerian goulash
   c) Welsh rarebit
   d) Scotch broth
   e) Irish stew
3. Which English earl gave his name to a well-known type of food? sandwich
4. Who dined on mince and slices of quince? owl & Pussy cat
5. In what country are cooked caterpillars regarded as a great wedding feast delicacy? new ginea
6. Which country is known as:
   a. The rice bowl country?
   b. The coffee pot country?
7. What are currants, raisins and sultanas? dryd fruit
8. Who is reputed to have said: "Let them eat cake!"
9. Which fruit did Persephone eat when she visited the Kingdom of Hades?
10. Which fruit, usually used as a vegetable, was once seldom eaten in America because it was considered poisonous?
11. What island is known as 'The Isle of Cloves'?
12. What was the nickname of the second Viscount Townshend, who did so much to help British agriculture?
13. What do the bells of St. Clement's say?

ANSWERS

1. Bananas.
2. a. French; b. Hungarian; c. Welsh; d. Scotch; e. Irish.
3. The Earl of Sandwich.
4. The owl and the pussycat.
5. New Guinea.
6. a. China; b. Brazil.
7. Different types of dried grapes.
8. Queen Marie Antoinette.
9. A pomegranate.
10. The tomato.
11. Zanzibar.
12. Turnip.
13. Oranges and Lemons.

Conjuring Capers

"Good heaven's, Spring, whatever are you dressed like that for?" gasped Billie, as she entered the den one morning and found Spring wearing a long, red cloak covered with stars, and a matching, pointed hat.

"Oh, he's not Spring this afternoon," grinned Doughnut. "He's Marvello, the marvellous magician. Sit down, Billie. The show is just about to begin. Spring is going to show us that he is just as good a conjuror as the one we saw at the Grand Theatre last night."

"This should be worth watching," cried Billie, as she took a seat in the front row. "Well, go ahead, Marvello, let's see your magic."

"Will some kind person in the audience lend me their watch?" asked Spring politely from the centre of the stage. "Come, sir, how about you?" he said, leaning forward and speaking directly to Scooper.

"Not likely," replied Scooper, "this watch was a birthday present, and I prefer to have time on my hands rather than on yours."

"Oh, give him a chance, Scooper," cried Brains, peering sympathetically at Spring through his glasses. "He can't show us any tricks if he has no props."

"Lend him *your* watch then," said Sticks with a wicked wink at the others.

"Oh . . . er . . . very well," replied Brains, handing over his watch very reluctantly. "But do take care, Spring, it's rather valuable."

"You mean it *was* valuable," replied Sticks as, with a mighty crash, Spring hit the watch with a heavy hammer.

"You idiot, what have you done?" wailed Brains. "Look at my watch, it's absolutely ruined!"

"Nonsense! When I have tapped it with my magic wand it will be as good as new," replied Spring confidently, suiting the action to his words.

But, although he continued to tap the watch for a further five minutes, all the works continued to hang out and the watch glass remained broken.

"I can't understand it at all," cried Spring. "I did exactly like Marvo the magician did last night, and not only did his watch become as good as new, but it also had a smart new strap on. I'm sorry, Brains, but even the best tricks go wrong, you know."

"You will be even more sorry when you get the repair bill for this watch," shouted Brains, as he stormed out of the den to see the watch repairer in the High Street.

The others started to get up, convinced that Spring would now abandon his show. But Marvello was still convinced of his own great skill as a magician.

"Don't leave, folks," he cried. "The show is only just beginning. Now, Scooper, please let me borrow that lovely white handkerchief for a

moment, and I will turn it a lovely blue shade to match your shirt."

Before Scooper was able to protest, Marvello had seized his best handkerchief and, while the rest of the Double Deckers watched in fascinated horror, Spring calmly dipped the pure silk handkerchief into a bottle of dark-blue ink.

"Wait until it dries and you will have a beautiful blue handkerchief," he said, smiling happily at Scooper, who gazed back at Spring as if he couldn't believe his ears, as Spring held the dripping piece of material aloft for all to see.

"That will never dry out properly in a month of Sundays," retorted Billie. "It is completely ruined, and please don't wave it about so, Spring, I don't want any ink on my new scarf. It took me ages to find the right colour and material."

"Yes, it *is* quite a pretty scarf," cried the magician, not one whit discomforted by the terrible glare Scooper gave him as he tossed the ink-soaked handkerchief into the dustbin. "But you know, Billie, long scarves are fashionable this year. Won't you let me try my magic and make it double its length?"

"Certainly not, you're a positive menace," cried Billie, clutching her scarf tightly. "Why don't you give up, Spring, and admit that you are no magician?"

"Well, of course, if that's the way you feel, there's no more to be said," said Spring haughtily. "Obviously I was wrong in thinking that a warm friendship existed between us."

"Oh, very well, take it," cried Billie resignedly, tossing the scarf up on the stage, while inwardly smiling at Spring's rather pompous choice of words. "But I warn you, Spring, if anything happens to my scarf, you buy me a new one."

"Billie, it worries me that you have such little faith in me," said Spring, as he calmly produced a large pair of scissors and proceeded to cut up Billie's beautiful scarf into ten tiny pieces.

"Oh, Spring, what have you done?" cried Billie, as the magician stuffed the pieces into a cardboard carton and started to chant a magical incantation, at the same time waving his wand over the carton.

"I have made you a beautiful, long scarf," replied Spring, as he confidently turned the carton upside down. "Oh . . . er . . . I'm afraid something seems to have gone wrong again," he murmured with a crestfallen smile, as all the bits merely tumbled out again, just as he had put them in.

"Well, that does it," murmured Scooper. "The show's over. Come along, everyone, let's all go for a game of cricket on the common."

"I'll join you when I have bought my new scarf," said Billie, with a glare at Spring. "Are you coming with me to help me choose it, Tiger?"

"No, I seem to have put Tiger down somewhere. I'd better look for him," said the youngest Double Decker with a worried frown, as she started to turn the den upside down looking for her mascot.

"Are *you* coming, Doughnut?" asked Scooper, hopefully, as he saw his plan for a cricket game quickly disappearing because of lack of players.

"When I've had a little rest," promised Doughnut lazily, as he popped a large sweet into his mouth.

As Scooper and Sticks gave up all thoughts of a cricket game and left the den, in disgust, for a short walk, a sudden gleam came into Spring's eye.

"If you feel like a little rest, try this couch," he suggested slyly to Doughnut.

"Gee, thanks," replied Doughnut sinking down on a strange, bedlike box and promptly falling asleep.

As Doughnut gave a little snore, Spring smiled, and drawing up the wooden back of the sofa, he swiftly turned it into a long box, with Doughnut's feet and head resting securely outside the box.

Suddenly Tiger, who was still searching for her pet mascot, gave a gasp of alarm. "Whatever are you doing to Doughnut?" she cried, as the

magician Double Decker reached down a rusty old sword from the wall. "Do be careful, that sword looks very dangerous."

"Nonsense, it may be a little rusty, but I am sure it will saw this box in half," replied Spring nonchalantly.

"But you might hurt Doughnut," squealed Tiger. "Doughnut, please wake up! Spring plans to saw you in two!"

"Well, this is one time when his plans will go awry," murmured Scooper, firmly. "Release Doughnut at once, Spring. Goodness knows what would have happened if it hadn't started to rain and Sticks and I hadn't cut short our walk."

"We would have had a really cut-up Doughnut," said Tiger, weak with relief, but still trying to make a little joke.

"I think that you are all making a big fuss about nothing," insisted Spring sulkily, as he helped a sleepy and bewildered Doughnut out of the box.

"What did you wake me up for?" asked Doughnut very indignantly. "I was having a wonderful dream. I dreamt that I went to an enchanted land where food grew on trees, and you could eat as much as you liked without being sick. The flowers were made from jellies, and there were doughnut trees and sausage bushes, and the pools and rivers were made of coke and ginger beer."

"It sounds a wonderful place," cried Tiger eagerly. "What a pity it was all a dream."

"Yes, but it was a dream that could easily have turned into a nightmare," insisted Scooper grimly, for he always felt responsible for the other Double Deckers. "Now, let's have an end of this conjuring lark once and for all, Spring, before something really serious happens."

"Oh, please, Scooper, let me try just one more trick," pleaded Spring. "It isn't the least bit dangerous. All I want to do is to show you all how to produce a rabbit from this old top-hat."

"Well, as long as you don't use that sword

to do it," agreed Scooper at last, very reluctantly. "And remember, Spring, this is the very last trick."

Spring nodded his head humbly as he waved his magic stick over the hat. "Abracadabra . . . one, two, three, I wave my wand, now what do you see?" he chanted.

The others craned forward in their seats, and Spring put his hand hopefully inside the hat.

His expression changed to one of triumph as his fingers touched something inside the hat. It felt soft to his fingers and he was sure, as he held it aloft, that it was the expected rabbit.

But, as a roar of laughter greeted him he looked up, and found that he was holding Tiger's pet mascot. "Oh, dear, not one of my tricks has gone right," he groaned sadly. "You were quite right, everybody, I will never make a conjuror."

But Tiger, who had been very worried at being unable to find her treasured toy, leaped onto the stage and threw her arms around Spring and hugged him hard. "Nonsense, this is a far better trick than pulling some silly old rabbit out of your hat," she declared, and she fondly hugged her little mascot. "I think that you are a very clever conjuror, Spring." And she glared down at the rest of the Double Deckers, as if daring them to disagree.

"Well, all's well that ends well," agreed Scooper. "Perhaps when you have had a few more lessons you can give us another show, Spring."

"Yes, but I'll make sure that sword isn't hanging around before you start," added Dough-nut, with a huge grin. "I think it would be rather awkward trying to eat, if I were cut in two!"

"Oh, I'm sure you'd manage to eat somehow," retorted Spring with a chuckle. "What do you all say to an ice cream now . . . my treat, of course!"

The deafening shout which greeted this question left Spring in no doubt as to their answer, and so the Double Deckers set off to produce a conjuring feat of their own—to make ice cream disappear in the shortest possible time!

STRANGE BUT TRUE

Toy spaniels have been favourites of royalty since Tudor times. The small 'dogge' of Mary Queen of Scots went with her to the executioner's block and was found, after she was beheaded, hiding in the folds of her gown.

Queen Elizabeth II of England has a giant among her ancestors! One of the Queen's forefathers was the emperor Charlemagne. He was a giant in stature —almost eight feet tall, and so strong that he could bend three horseshoes out of shape with one hand.

Wyatt Earp, the famous gun-fighting U.S. marshal of Dodge City and Tombstone, was a boxing referee. Among other fights, he refereed the heavyweight bout between Bob Fitzsimmons and Tom Sharkey in San Francisco on 2nd December 1896, before a crowd of 15,000. He wore his famous buntline '45.

Captain Matthew Webb, familiar to millions as 'the man on the match box', was the first man to swim the Channel without aid, in 1875. He swam the breast-stroke for 22 hours. To celebrate his feat, a famous firm used him as their box top design. He once said that he could stay longer in the sea than a Newfoundland dog. He tried it, and won easily—the dog almost died. Although suffering from ill-health at the time, he attempted to swim across Niagara Falls. He almost succeeded, but was sucked into the whirlpool and never seen again.

Lord's Cricket Ground is believed by many to have at some time been associated with aristocratic teams, but the name in fact has nothing to do with peers. It is named after Thomas Lord, who ~~laid~~ down the *first* ground on the site of what is now Dorset Square, Marylebone.

The word 'Strike', all too familiar in newspapers, originated in the old days of sail. It was first used in its modern sense in 1768 and was applied to seamen with a grievance. Refusing to sail, they lowered (struck) the yards of their ship.

Double Deckers' DOTTY DOG CHASE!

Brains has done it again! Follow the Double Deckers in a wild chase across London in pursuit of Brains' latest invention — a mechanical flying dog! An accidental press on the switch has sent the crazy canine careering across the city, and the Double Deckers are scared at just what the robot dog might get up to, especially with Brains attached to his stout chain lead!

To join the hunt, you will need a counter for each of the players and a dice. Each player must throw a six to start and then the race is on! The winner is the first person to arrive at the scene of the canine's latest crime and Brains' final disgrace! But remember that you have to obey the special instructions in some of the squares, if you happen to land on one of these.

11
12
13
14
7
8
9
HITCH A RIDE ON ALBERT'S CART TAKE A SHORT CUT.
CATCH SIGHT OF ROBOT DOG WITH BRAINS IN TOW. MOVE ON 3 SQUARES
16
23
CAUGHT IN TRAFFIC JAM MISS 1 TURN.
21
20
19
18
17
24
44
45
DOUGHNUT HAS GOT BEHIND. GO BACK 3 SQUARES
43
47
SHAKE A 6 TO RESCUE BRAINS AND STOP DOG.
41
SHORT CUT BY THE TOWER OF LONDON.
48
53
49
50
51
52

a DRUM for STICKS

Working on his latest experiment in his lab in the Double Deckers' den, Brains suddenly heard a crash, then a tearing sound, and then a great shout of anger.

He went out to investigate and was just in time to see Doughnut gingerly removing his foot from out of Sticks' drum.

"Gosh, Sticks, I'm sorry," gasped Doughnut in dismay. "I didn't see your drum in this dark corner."

"No, because you were too busy filling your great big mouth full of jammy doughnuts," cried Sticks angrily, as he surveyed the damage to his beloved drum. "You are a great, big, fat oaf! And you're no longer any friend of mine."

"Now, steady on, Sticks," said Scooper, putting a comforting hand on his friend's shoulder, and also seeing that Doughnut looked very upset. "It was a real accident, you know. Perhaps we can get your drum repaired."

"No hope of that!" replied Sticks sadly. "It would cost as much as buying a new one."

"Well, we shall have to do just that," said Billie briskly. "Money will be the problem, of course. How much can we raise between us?"

Everyone searched their pockets. But as it was the end of the week the result was not very encouraging . . . four shillings, two buttons, a space coin disc and, very surprisingly, one French franc.

"Where did that come from?" asked Scooper in surprise.

"Oh, it's one we used during our project on France," replied Tiger, whose contribution it was. "I brought it home to show you."

"Well, it's very interesting, but it won't help towards a new drum," said Brains. "We shall have to think of some way of raising more money."

"Perhaps we could have a flag day?" suggested Spring. "A 'buy a flag for a drum' day."

"It's illegal to do that unless you are collecting for a charity," Brains said immediately.

"Surely this is a case of charity beginning at home," said Spring wittily. "We could always put on a show and raise money that way," he added. "I could do my Sammy Davis act. It's sure to bring the house down."

"The way you dance would bring the Festival Hall down. It's like a stampede of elephants," cried Doughnut cheekily.

"Well, of course, *you* know all about elephants, being a first cousin of the animals," retorted Spring.

"Listen, I've just remembered something," cried Tiger, eager to prevent another quarrel. "I saw a notice in the High Street saying that the local dairies are running special competitions to promote their goods. Tomorrow there is to be an egg and spoon race down the High Street with a cash prize for the winner. Let's all have a go. And if any of us wins, the money will buy Sticks a new drum."

"Good for you, young Tiger," cried Billie admiringly. "You may be a tiddler, but you're always hitting the jackpot with your ideas."

"Didn't you know that all the best goods come in small parcels?" said Tiger with a laugh, and she hit Spring with her mascot as he mimed 'big head' at her.

So, next morning, all the Double Deckers arrived early at the starting point to take their spoons and china eggs from Dan the dairyman.

"You've got some strong competition over there, Scooper," said Dan, as he gave the Double Decker his egg and spoon.

Scooper looked in the direction where Dan was pointing, and he groaned. "Basher Brown and his gang," he murmured to himself. "They are always up to underhand tricks when there's money at stake. Just look how cockily Basher is holding his spoon. I'm sure he's stuck his egg on with chewing gum."

But before he could go and challenge Basher, the starter called out for all competitors to come to the starting tape.

"I think I'll drop out of the race and keep my eye on Basher," he whispered to the rest of the Double Deckers. "Just take it slow and steady, and watch out for Basher's gang."

At first all went well, as Brains and Sticks headed the field, closely followed by Basher Brown and his chief crony, Bill Black. Billie and Tiger were well to the back, but each taking care not to drop the china egg.

"Keep it up, girls, you're doing fine," encouraged Scooper, as he passed them on the side of the pavement.

But he was just in time to see Bill Black deliberately put out a foot, causing Brains to stumble and drop his egg.

"Yah, you're out!" jeered Bill, as he passed Brains. "You Double Deckers don't stand a chance!"

"Not if that's how they mean to play," said Scooper grimly to Brains, who had joined him on the pavement. "Look, Brains, Basher's gang have deliberately got rid of all the other competitors except us. We shall have to start using their tactics if we mean to get that drum for Sticks."

"I quite agree with you," replied Brains seriously, as he began to systematically turn out his pockets. "This is one time that the end justifies the means. It's a good job I fill my pockets with an emergency kit. Look, this drum of pepper, this miniature horn and these tin tacks are sure to come in useful."

"Then let's get going!" cried Scooper. "Look, one of the gang has just offered Doughnut a cream cake. That's the end of *him* in the race."

"Yes, and he tried to take my tiger away from me," said a sad little voice. "I had to hit him over the head with it to stop him, but it lost me my place in the race."

"Cheer up, young Tiger, he tripped me up too," said Brains. "Gather round, everyone, and I'll give you the plan of action. Basher Brown's gang is about to meet its doom."

There was a hurried conference, and then each of the defeated Double Deckers ran off, each with a definite object.

Tiger was the first to go into action. She waited until Bill Black and his young brother were just in front of her and then, making sure that nobody else saw her, she sprinkled a box of tin tacks straight in their path.

As the two Blacks stepped on to the tin tacks and they penetrated their running pumps, Bill's and Bob's cries of pain could be heard down the whole length of the High Street.

"It's not fair, some rotter has put tin tacks on the road," squealed Bill, as he hopped about on one foot in a vain attempt to stop his egg falling off his spoon. "I'm sure it was one of those cheeky Double Deckers."

"Yes, it was," insisted Bob, as he helped his brother on to the pavement. "But there's no sign of Tiger now, and we should never be able to prove it. Never mind, there's still some of our gang in the race and only one Double Decker. Harry pushed Billie out of the way and she fell, and he knocked Spring's arm so that he dropped his egg."

"Tee-hee," laughed Bill, "I wish I could have seen it."

"You'll be laughing on the other side of your face before the race is finished," murmured Scooper, as he sprinkled pepper on a large handkerchief. "Things are going to get evened up a little in a minute."

To the casual onlooker it just appeared that he chose that moment to cheer the runners on with his handkerchief. But actually, Scooper, with skilful timing, waved the handkerchief just as Johnny Green was passing by.

The pepper on the handkerchief was blown about in the air and a whiff of the pepper went right up Johnny's nose.

"Atishoo! Atishoo!" Johnny sneezed, as he wobbled about and his egg fell to the ground with a crash.

"Another down, just two to go, and good old Sticks still going strong," murmured Scooper, as he wisely disappeared into the midst of the crowd. "I hope Brains can find old Bonzo."

Brains had been searching all over for Tom Brown's dog, and at last he had found him, sitting patiently outside the butcher's shop waiting for a bone.

Searching his pockets for any spare coins, Brains just managed to scrape up enough money for a large, juicy bone.

"Come along, Bonzo," he called softly, and he used the bone to entice the dog back into the High Street.

Little by little, Brains drew Bonzo almost to the end of the finishing line, and then he led him to the edge of the pavement. Then, just as Tom Brown drew level, he squeezed hard on the horn.

Honk! Honk!

Startled, Tom looked where the noise was coming from, and in a trice, Brains threw the bone to him. Tom caught it automatically with one hand and, at the same moment, Bonzo recognized his master.

With a joyful growl, Bonzo leapt off the pavement, and Tom, his dog, the bone, and the egg and spoon rolled in a confused heap onto the ground.

"Now there's only Sticks and Basher in the race," cried Tiger to the others, as she jumped up and down in glee. "Sticks is sure to beat him, like he did in the school sports."

But the rest of the Double Deckers exchanged worried glances.

"Basher won't give up without a fight," said Brains. "He'll do anything to stop Sticks from winning."

"Look, you're right," cried Doughnut indignantly, as the two runners came into view. "Did you see that? Basher deliberately kicked Sticks on the ankle. Poor old Sticks, he's hopping about in pain."

"Yes, but he's still managed to hold on to his egg and spoon," cried Billie. "So he's still in the race."

"Yes, but he will only be able to hobble now, and watch Basher streak away with that triumphant grin on his face," moaned Spring. "Oh, there's no justice in the world. So near and yet so far!"

But, just at that moment, fortune decided to smile on the Double Deckers after all for, suddenly, the chewing gum which Basher *had* used to stick his egg to his spoon, finally worked loose.

Basher, of course, did not realise this and, barely a couple of inches from the tape, he decided to show off. With a smug grin he turned his spoon upside down, confident that the egg was secure, but it rolled off. And with it went all Basher's hopes of winning the race.

Forgetting in his rage that it was a china egg, Basher kicked it hard, but his cries of pain were lost in the cheers of the crowd as Sticks hobbled gallantly over the finishing line to be proclaimed the winner.

"I never thought I'd win," cried Sticks, as the others crowded around to congratulate him. "It seems like magic, the way things kept happening to Basher's gang. It was certainly my lucky day."

"Well, sometimes Lady Luck needs a little help," murmured Billie, as she used her handkerchief to put a cold compress on Sticks' ankle.

Sticks looked surprised as the others all started to laugh. But he was delighted as Dan came over with two crisp five pound notes as his prize.

"What are you going to buy with the money?" Dan asked, with a smile.

"Oh, a new drum," replied Sticks at once. And then he added, with a chuckle, as he saw Basher Brown and his gang glaring at him from the pavement: "And I might buy a bunch of sweet grapes for Basher and his gang. Their expressions show that they have a bad case of sour grapcs at thc moment."

And, helped by his friends, Sticks hobbled off to buy himself the best drum in the music shop.

That night the Double Deckers held a celebration so that Sticks could try out his new drum.

Billie and Doughnut danced the *pas-de-deux* of thc Egg and Spoon; Spring and Scooper exchanged clever yolk jokes and, as the grand finale, Sticks composed his Basher's Downfall Concerto for drums only, a magnificent piece of music which Basher's gang heard way down the street and which turned them red with rage and then green with envy.

"We'll get our own back one day," vowed Basher, shaking his fist at the junkyard where the Double Deckers were celebrating . . . but *they* were too happy to care!

Do you think that buses are just another form of transport, or are you like a growing number of people who have turned their love of buses into an interesting and rewarding hobby?

BUS SPOTTING CAN BE FUN!

ENTHUSIASTS' CLUBS

Bus spotting clubs have sprung up all over the British Isles over the last twenty years. Here, fellow enthusiasts can meet to talk, watch films, swop fleet lists and make regular visits to other towns to see interesting buses and places of interest.

Among the thriving clubs are the Ribble Enthusiasts' Club in Lancashire, one of the earliest ever formed, the Southdown Enthusiasts' Club, and the Shamrock and Rambler Enthusiasts' Club.

TICKET COLLECTING

The tickets issued by the various bus companies are of great interest to a bus spotter. There are many different kinds such as TIM, Ultimate, Willibrew, Bell Punch and Bellgraphic, and although most spotters like to travel on certain buses themselves and obtain these tickets at first hand, it is possible to exchange or buy tickets through the columns of such magazines as *Buses,* published monthly by Ian Allen.

Details of the tickets are usually entered up in notebooks and the tickets themselves kept in envelopes.

PHOTOGRAPHS AND STAMPS

Some enthusiasts who are also keen photographers like to keep a photographic record of the buses they have seen, supplementing their collection with official photographs, which can be easily bought.

Another offshoot of this hobby is the collecting of stamps featuring buses, such as the colourful bus stamp, illustrated in great detail, and issued by the Moroccan government. A quick eye will spot the left-hand side mirror, the correct position for a country keeping to the right of the road.

This is the last Tiger Cub ever built. It has a Fowler body and a front entrance.

This bus is one of only two ever built especially for the route up Great Orme in North Wales.

The only type now running in public service in Britain, this Albion-Venturer was first built in 1948.

CODES AND CIPHERS

To the ordinary public who scarcely give the numbers and letters on the side of a bus a second glance, these mean very little, but a seasoned spotter can read the code in a second.

Single-deck bus B
Single-deck coach C
Single-deck dual-purpose bus/coach DP
Double-deck highbridge with centre gangways H
Double-deck lowbridge with sunken side gangway on upper deck L
F—Front entrance
C—Centre entrance
E—Rear entrance
R—Rear
Dua-Front and rear entrances D

So B44F is a single-deck bus, seating 44 people, and it has a front entrance, while CH41/27 D is a coach, highbridge with a seating capacity of forty-one seats on top deck and twenty-seven on lower deck and front and rear entrances.

FLEET LISTS AND TIMETABLES

Enthusiasts buy and sell, and often swop fleet lists of different companies, eager to keep up to date with recent acquisitions or vehicles withdrawn from service.

New registration numbers are eagerly sought after and recorded on fleet lists, and new types of buses are quickly recognised when they first appear on the roads.

Another part of the bus spotter's hobby is collecting timetables from every available bus service in the country. Not only are these of great interest to the enthusiast, but they are also very useful to other members of his family at holiday times, or merely to check the time of the next local bus.

So, if you are looking for a new and very interesting hobby, take a bus to fun and adventure! You will make lots of friends, see plenty of interesting places . . . and never be late for a bus!

LUCKY MASCOT

The youngest Double Decker will never be parted from her lucky tiger mascot, and there have been many similar mascots which their owners staunchly believe bring luck or happiness, and they fear that misfortune would follow if they lost them.

THE MISSING BLACK CAT

Records tell us that King Charles I was a very superstitious person; he believed that all his good fortune during his reign was brought about by the black cat which was his frequent companion.

This cat was a greatly favoured member of the royal household, and he was closely guarded whenever his royal master was unable to be present to look after the animal himself.

When this cat vanished from the royal apartments one day and could not be found, Charles was both inconsolable and very apprehensive, publicly avowing that at last his luck had deserted him. Although his courtiers tried to reassure him, the king's prophecy proved correct, for a short time later he was arrested and sent for trial.

SIMON OF THE 'AMETHYST'

Another cat, Simon, the mascot of H.M.S. *Amethyst,* helped to keep the crew in good spirits when their ship was attacked by Chinese communists in May 1949, as the *Amethyst* was taking supplies up river to the British Embassy.

Although wounded by shrapnel and badly shell-shocked, gallant old Simon continued to keep the hundreds of rats at bay which had begun to swarm all over the decks searching for food as the frigate was forced to anchor for several weary months. The surviving members of the crew were heartily cheered by this practical display of duty, and later Simon was the first cat ever to receive the Dickin Medal, the Animals' V.C.

THE NAUGHTY BEARS

All the armed forces have their own regimental mascots which head official parades, and at the turn of this century mascots of the Royal Navy included Bruno the bear.

One day Bruno escaped, and before he was recaptured this mischievous animal had climbed aboard a visiting ship and pulled down the ship's flag, much to the embarrassment of the Admiralty authorities.

FUR AND FEATHER MASCOTS

In contrast, the parrot taken by Thor Heyerdahl on his Kontiki expedition was very well-behaved, as was a black cat named Georgina who was a member of the crew of H.M.S. *Ulster* during the war, sharing with them the dangers in the D-Day landings and, when things were quieter, playing table-tennis with the sailors.

Tirpitz was the pig mascot of a German cruiser, and the only survivor when the ship was sunk. He raised several pounds for charity and today, his head is on view, in London's Imperial War Museum.

Bulldogs were naturally popular mascots for 'the bulldog breed', and these included Windsor of H.M.S. *Repulse,* who spent his leave ashore standing outside butchers' shops, and Joey who liked a tot of rum aboard H.M.S. *Queen Elizabeth,* two ships which saw gallant action during World War I.

In 1968, Joey, who on his death had been stuffed, became the mascot of a new survey ship, H.M.S. *Bulldog.*

THE CROWING COCK

Another creature, this time a cock—part of a ship's provisions—was instrumental in rallying the dispirited men of H.M.S. *Marlborough* during the war between France and England in the late eighteenth century.

It was on the 'Glorious First of June' that this ship got into difficulties, due to her senior officers being seriously wounded, and the crew were actually beginning to think of surrendering to the French when they heard the loud, triumphant crowing of a cock.

There it perched on the broken mainmast, crowing triumphantly, as if calling the men once more to arms. To a man the sailors responded to this cocky young bird and engaged the enemy in battle once again—this time to turn the tide of disaster into a wonderful victory.

All praise was given to the proud cock, who became the revered mascot of the ship. He never saw the stewpot for which he was intended, but instead was fussed over by the delighted crew. He later became a pet in a nobleman's household, where he lived until his death.

SAILORS' MASCOTS

Although today many ships have a cat mascot, long ago the figurehead at the prow of the boat was thought by sailors to be their own lucky mascot.

These figureheads were carved with great care, for they were believed by superstitious sailors to be the ship's guardians, who would watch over them when danger threatened.

In Greek mythology, when Jason asked Argo to build him a ship in which to search for the Golden Fleece, the figurehead Argo fashioned was the face of Hera, wife of Zeus, who had promised Jason she would give her protection to the expedition. When—as a result of a foolish action on the part of Hercules—a great god picked up Jason's ship and wrecked it, the first object Jason sought to recover from the waves was Hera's image.

Other figureheads probably have just as interesting tales woven around their origin. A Cornish smuggler had two cheeky golden cherubs designed for his ship, while a ship built in 1848 and wrecked during a gale—as she carried a cargo of herrings through the Straits of Gibraltar to Italy—had an English huntsman holding a fox's brush.

Florence Nightingale did much to help the soldiers during the Crimean War, so no doubt sailors thought that this was a good enough reason to have *her* figurehead on the prows of their ships.

SPORTS' MASCOTS

Many sportsmen have a mascot which they feel brings them luck in their chosen game. Footballer Jackie Milburn always felt that he played a good game when his lucky elephant mascot was sewn securely into the waistband of his shorts, and a certain seaside club always won whenever a seagull perched on their goalposts.

A northern club once adopted a caged magpie as its mascot, but this proved very unlucky, and the bird made only one appearance on the pitch before being banished. But, as one very old spectator was heard to remark: "'Twas a foolish thing to do. Everyone knows a lone magpie brings sorrow, and we were sure to lose the match!"

Many footballers have a pair of boots which they consider their lucky mascots, and even when the boots are worn out they may still hang in the players' dressing-room to bring their team luck.

Karen Muir, a young South African girl swimmer who made history by becoming a world record holder at the age of twelve when she won the hundred-and-ten yards backstroke, had a favourite teddy bear which she took with her to swimming events, and which seemed to bring her luck. Her mascot was the first thing Karen wanted to hold after winning a race.

More recently, a lion mascot named Winston accompanied Sir Francis Chichester on his epic voyage in *Gypsy Moth II,* and shared in the triumphant return.

So if you have a mascot, treat it kindly, because one day it may bring you luck when you least expect it!

IT'S A SCOOP!

A cold and rainy day has kept the Double Deckers indoors, and so Scooper has worked out all these puzzles for the gang to do. Why don't you join in the fun?

1. Which is correct? Five and four *is* ten or five and four *are* ten?

2. All these are countries of the world, but as you can see, some of their letters are missing. Do you know what the countries are?

GerMaNy	AMERica
FRANcE	HOLLaNd
EngLaNd	AfRiCA
BelGiUm	SWITZeRLaND

3. Still with travel in mind, do you know which flag a ship hoists when it is about to sail?

The Blue Peter

4. With the help of these drawings you should be able to fill in the missing letters and so find out the names of four birds:

a. CanARY b. bullFINCH

c. PenGUIN d. PeaCOCK

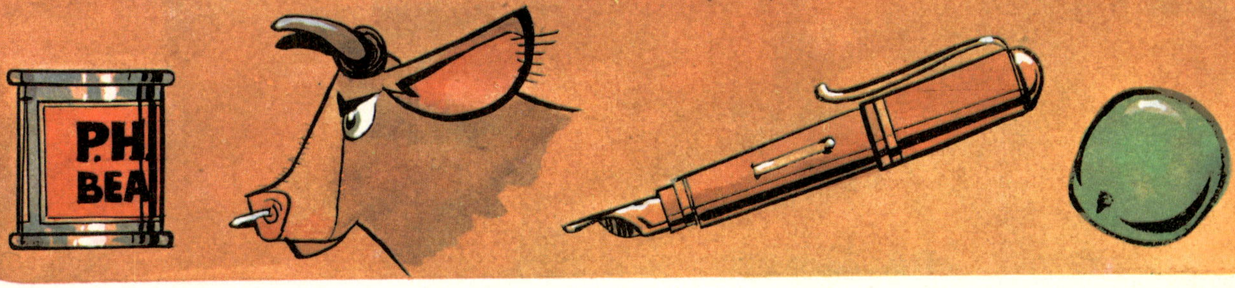

5. Doughnut has lost sight of his favourite dish. A banana, chocolate, nut, raspberry, topped with whipped cream, sundae. It seems to be at the end of this maze; can you help him find his way through?

6. Take two of these matches away, so that you only have two squares left.

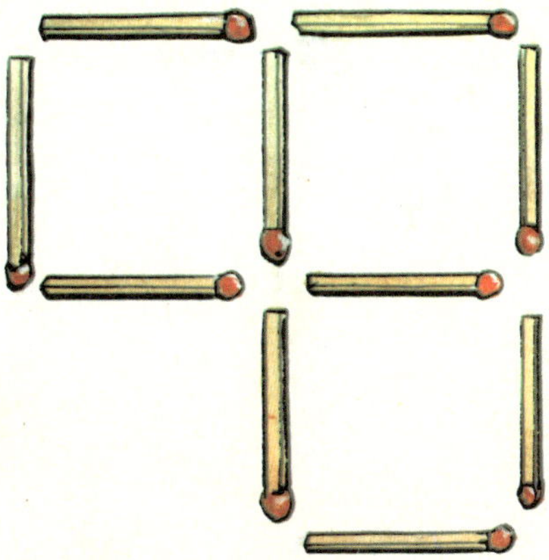

ANSWERS

1. Neither, the answer's nine!
2. Germany; America; France; Holland; England; Africa; Belgium; Switzerland.
3. The Blue Peter.
4. a. Canary; b. Bullfinch; c. Penguin; d. Peacock.
6. Remove the two matches in the upper right-hand corner.

Doughnut's Diet

"Gosh, Doughnut, this is the first time I have ever seen you come into the den without a cake in your hand," cried Tiger, in tones of great astonishment. "Don't you feel well?"

"Er . . . er . . . yes, I'm quite well, thanks," replied Doughnut. But he looked very uncomfortable, and he tried to hide the book which he was carrying under his arm from the interested gaze of the rest of the Double Deckers.

But Billie's quick eyes had already spotted the title, and she said with a chuckle: "One hundred easy diets. Are you really trying to lose a few pounds at last? Well, it's about time."

"A few pounds . . . more like a few stones," cried Spring, cheekily. "He must weigh more than a baby elephant."

"Hey, steady on," retorted Doughnut good-naturedly. "Actually, the real reason for the diet is because the park-keeper says I can't go on the boating lake again until I lose some weight. He's afraid I might sink one of his boats," he finished with a sheepish grin.

The other Double Deckers roared with laughter when they heard this. But Tiger said sympathetically: "I think it's a splendid idea, Doughnut. Which diet are you going to try?"

"I haven't made up my mind yet," confessed Doughnut. "There are so many to choose from, and some of them are very expensive."

"Well, here's a good one, which will be both cheap and nourishing," said Billie, who had been glancing through the book. "Milk and bananas several times a day, Doughnut. You love bananas, and I know you can drink milk until it comes out of your ears."

"Yes, I'll try that one," cried Doughnut, his face brightening. "It sounds better than lettuce leaves and lemon juice," he added with a chuckle. "I'll go and stock up with bananas and milk now."

"And we'll come with you, just to make sure that you don't call in at the cake shop on the way," said Scooper and Spring firmly, as Brains opened the door to let Doughnut out.

For the first day Doughnut found his dieting was quite pleasant for, as Billie said, he did like both bananas and milk, and his friends encouraged him to eat only what the book ordered.

But on the second day the food did not taste quite as good, and Spring and Sticks kept teasing Doughnut.

"If you eat any more bananas you'll end up swinging from tree to tree," grinned Spring, as he peeled the wrapper from a large block of chocolate.

"Yeh, look how hairy your arms are growing," added Sticks, with a wicked smile. "Are you quite sure you haven't started growing a tail yet?"

Doughnut began to look quite alarmed and Billie took up the cudgels on his behalf. "I know a couple of monkeys who haven't got tails, but who might get a couple of black eyes if they don't shut up," she warned.

Knowing that Billie could be quite a tomboy when she wished and that she was quite handy with her fists, Spring and Sticks wisely said no more. But they made a silent mime of monkey antics behind Billie's back which did nothing to allay Doughnut's fears.

However, just at that moment, Scooper arrived back with the news that both the fruiterer

and the dairy were completely sold out because of Doughnut's heavy demands.

"I'm afraid that's the end of that diet, old man," said Scooper and, although Doughnut tried to look suitably disappointed, both Tiger and Billie realised that secretly Doughnut was rather pleased, and very relieved.

"Well, we shall just have to think of another way to lose weight, if you don't feel like going on another diet right away," said Scooper. "Now, personally, I feel that there's nothing like a bit of exercise to lose a bit of weight. Sticks, Spring and I could take you on a cross-country run a couple of mornings every week."

"Well, alright, if you think it might work," said Doughnut, looking rather doubtful.

"Early morning is best, about six o'clock," said Spring, winking at the others. "Cheer up, Doughnut, it's all in a good cause," he added, as his fat friend collapsed on the floor in horror at the prospect. "We'll meet on the common at six sharp tomorrow morning . . . shorts and singlets, of course."

So, for the next few mornings, Scooper, Sticks and Spring, accompanied several yards behind by Doughnut, ran along the common for five miles before breakfast.

"Poor old Doughnut, here he comes at last, puffing away like a walrus," said Scooper, as their plump Double Decker chum came into sight at last. "He's been a real brick the way he has come on these early morning runs with us."

"Yeh, but don't you think it strange that he has not lost any weight at all?" said Sticks with a puzzled frown. "We have all lost a couple of pounds, according to the scales, but Doughnut hasn't lost one single ounce. It is one of the minor mysteries of life."

"But one which I think we are about to solve," cried Spring. "Look, we all wondered why he insisted on carrying that rucksack on his back each day. I have only just realised that it looks full at the start of the run but now it is quite empty."

"And this morning the old rogue hasn't completely wiped his face clean of the jam and cream!" cried Scooper. "Come here, Doughnut,

have you been eating doughnuts?" he cried sternly.

"Only to keep up my strength for our early morning runs," persisted Doughnut. "Honestly, fellas, without them I would have fainted right away."

"And we thought you were being extra virtuous when you refused an extra rasher and an egg when Billie cooked our breakfast back in the den," shouted Spring angrily. "I can see we have all been wasting our time."

"Well, Brains must come up with one of *his* bright ideas," said Scooper, as the quartet made their way back to the den. "And I shall tell Billie that *you* have already had your breakfast," he added, turning to Doughnut with a stern frown.

"I was only trying to keep up my strength," Doughnut kept murmuring as he trudged disconsolately behind the others on their way back to their Double Decker den in the junkyard.

"Of course, all this is really a question of mind over matter," said Brains rather pompously as he peered at Doughnut through his glasses after Spring had poured out the result of the cross-country runs. "You will just have to stop *thinking* about food, that's all. You must try and eat nothing at all for a day. Just sit quietly, thinking happy thoughts, and the time will pass quickly."

Even Spring and Scooper looked extremely doubtful at this advice, but Tiger urged Doughnut to give it a try. "Think of all the fun you have on the boating lake," she said, in an attempt to spur him on to make the effort.

"Oh, very well, I'll give it a try, just for this morning," said Doughnut resignedly, as he sat down in a corner.

But, unfortunately for Brains' plan, all Doughnut could think about was food. In his mind's eye he saw doughnuts filled with jam and cream, bottles of sweets, plates of thick treacle pudding, and even semolina pudding, which usually he hated.

And when Scooper heard the ice cream man's bell and went off to get some for everyone, Doughnut gave a terrible groan and gave up completely, especially when Scooper had forgotten about the diet and had bought a cone for Doughnut out of force of habit.

"Gosh, that tasted smashing," cried Doughnut, as he finished his ice cream a full five minutes before the others.

"Yes, but it won't help you to lose weight," said Billie. "Now, Doughnut, *I* keep my trim figure by dancing. How about trying a spot of the light fantastic, as they say, to solve your weight problem?"

"This I must see," chuckled Spring, as Billie led a reluctant Doughnut out into the yard for his first lesson. "Talk about the dance of the sugar plum fairy—this will seem more like the stampede of the baby elephant," he chuckled, as they all piled out to watch the dancers.

But, to everyone's great astonishment, Doughnut was found to be surprisingly light on his feet. He followed Billie's rather intricate foot patterns without making one single mistake.

"Why, Doughnut, that was marvellous!" cried Billie, as she stopped for a moment. "You're a born dancer. Now, let's see what you can do by yourself."

So, with the aid of Sticks on the drums, Doughnut evolved a very clever clowning act, combining some knockabout comedy with some neat dancing.

As Doughnut took a bow at the end of the act, his friends burst into a round of spontaneous applause.

"Gee, that was terrific, Doughnut!" cried Sticks. "How about me and you teaming up as a double act?"

"No. If he's going to partner anyone, it's going to be me," retorted Billie firmly. "After all, it was me who suggested giving Doughnut dancing lessons."

They were all so busy arguing about who was going to cash in on Doughnut's talents that they failed to notice the large man walking in through the gates.

"Hello there, kids," he said, talking loudly with a large cigar still clenched between his teeth. "I've just been watching your little show

and was very impressed. I'm producing the local pantomime down at the Royal Theatre, and . . ."

"I'm a good dancer," interrupted Billie eagerly.

"And I can play the drums," cried Sticks, not to be outdone.

"Sorry, kids, all the parts are booked," said the man, with a regretful smile. "All, that is, except one," he added and he gave Doughnut a long, thoughtful stare.

"How do you fancy being Father Bear in my Goldilocks pantomime?" he said at last to Doughnut. "The actor I engaged has just gone sick, and I am finding it very difficult to get a replacement. The folk who can dance are not fat enough for the role. But this young fellow will fit the part admirably. What do you say?"

"He says 'yes', of course," Billie replied firmly, seeing that for once in his life Doughnut was completely speechless.

"Well, report tomorrow morning at the stage door at nine o'clock sharp," said the producer, as he turned to go. "And don't go losing any weight between now and the start of the show. You need every pound you've got for this part. In fact, here you are, I'll give you a cake allowance, starting right now. Go and buy as many cakes as you can eat . . . and buy some for your friends, too."

"Gosh, why are you looking so glum, Doughnut?" asked Billie, as they watched the man enter a great big limousine. "It's a terrific part. We all envy you."

"But now I won't be able to slim and I shan't be able to go on the boating lake," wailed Doughnut.

"Why, with the money you will make for your part in the pantomime you will be able to buy a boat of your own," laughed Billie. "And we'll all come and cheer you in the show."

"Will you?" cried Doughnut, his face brightening up. "Well, you know, I don't really mind about the boat. Perhaps I'll buy a racing car instead."

"Well, before you do, let's buy those doughnuts," pleaded Tiger. "Remember what the producer said about keeping fat . . . er, I mean pleasantly rounded," she said quickly, as Doughnut gave her a glare.

So off they went, and bought up the baker's entire stock of cakes. "Please make up the same order for tomorrow," said Doughnut grandly, as he threw the money carelessly on the counter.

"You must eat like a horse," said the baker, as he watched Doughnut tuck into a delicious jammy doughnut.

"No, like a bear," replied Doughnut gravely, and the baker scratched his head in bewilderment as all the Double Deckers went into roars of laughter at Doughnut's witty reply.

The show was a great success and Doughnut took six curtain calls, to the delight of his friends, who watched the show from the best box in the house. But how they laughed when, after Doughnut had presented Goldilocks with a lovely bouquet of flowers, the actress returned the compliment with a large box of doughnuts!

MUSICAL MISCELLANY

The composer Christian Wolff recently composed a score called STICKS, which is actually played with percussion instruments and sticks only, making an entirely new musical sound.

On special feast days in Mexico drummers play special dog-shaped horizontal drums known as *teponaztli,* some of which are hundreds of years old.

Before London's Big Ben strikes the hour, a short piece of music, taken from Handel's *Messiah,* is played.

The famous composer Haydn once gave a new composition to his butcher's daughter as a wedding present, and in gratitude the butcher sent Haydn an ox, decorated with flowers and vine leaves. It was led to the composer's home in the middle of the night by a band of musicians playing the very air which Haydn had just composed.

During the time of Brian Boru, High King of Ireland, the harpist was a man of esteemed rank at court, and his harp was a very valuable instrument. Today a golden harp represents Northern Ireland on the British royal coat of arms.

Scotland is famous for its bagpipes, and although famous Scottish regiments are justly proud of their pipe bands, and Her Majesty the Queen has her own personal piper who plays for her at breakfast during her holidays up north, bagpipes first appeared over two thousand years ago in the Middle East.

The Greek god Pan played such sweet music that his sheep never strayed away. Pan's pipes were made from reeds cut in varying lengths and tied together, and were known as a *syrinx.*

There have been bellringer societies as far back as the sixteenth century. Bellringers are known as campanologists, and when bells are struck in a regular order this is known as a *round,* and during a peal of bells there are at least five thousand *changes,* none of which should be repeated.

Did you know that the fine lady who went to Banbury riding a cock horse was believed to be the first Queen Elizabeth? At that time it was the fashion to have tiny bells at the end of ladies' long, pointed shoes. And since the horses were also bedecked with bells and the queen loved musicians to play to her on long journeys, she certainly had music wherever she went, as the rhyme truly says.

BRAINS' BOOK OF KNOWLEDGE

The Double Deckers gave Brains a book for his birthday, telling him that he would find facts inside which would remind him of each of them— and, to his great surprise, he did!

STICK INSECTS look just like dried-up twigs and, unlike most other insects, they have no wings. They would make interesting, if rather unusual pets, and could be easily kept on a piece of privet hedge, as they are very hungry leafeaters.

The brontosaurus, which lived some fifteen million years ago, is believed to have had the smallest BRAIN of any living creature, but it also had a secondary brain in its sacral vertebrae which was several times larger than the brain in its head.

One of the contents of an Australian workman's swagbag was his BILLY. This was a tin used as a kettle, to boil water for a drink to refresh him on his long walks through the outback, as he travelled from cattle station to sheep farm, seeking work.

The TIGER, a large member of the cat family, has keen senses, and although an excellent hunter, will only attack a man if it is hungry or angry. But tigers eat thousands of sheep and cattle each year in Asia and India. The Bengal tiger has long, narrow stripes, black in colour; the Caucasian tiger has brown stripes, and the Siberian tiger has longer hair, much lighter in colour because of its living climate.

A SCOOPER is a kind of avocet, which is a long-legged wading bird with black and white plumage, and it has a long flat beak which curves upwards, thus allowing the bird to collect small water creatures by scraping its beak along shallow pools. Some people believe that avocets 'talk' to each other by moving their heads in different ways.

On 'Trick or Treat' night in the United States, children dress up and visit friends and neighbours, threatening to play light-hearted tricks on them if the people refuse to give the children a small present such as sweets, fruits or DOUGHNUTS.

There is an old legend which says that the first day of SPRING is the traditional day on which the birds choose their yearly king. This honour falls upon the bird that can fly nearest to the sun and, because of its powerful wings it is usually the eagle which achieves this.

But, one year, a clever little wren, weighing only a few ounces, perched, unknown to the retiring king, on top of his head. Thus, in theory, the wren was nearer to the sun and so became King of the Birds for that year!

SEASIDE ADVENTURE

"Say, Scooper, this is a great idea of yours to come for a day trip to the seaside," cried Spring enthusiastically, as he and the rest of the Double Deckers made their way to the station exit after getting off the excursion train.

"Hey, wait for me," called a familiar voice. "It was bad enough having to travel all the way in the guard's van without being left behind once we have got here."

"Sorry, Albert," cried Scooper, throwing an arm around his friend's shoulders. "We were so eager to get down to the beach that I'm afraid we forgot all about you."

"That's a fine thing," grumbled Albert.

But he was a good-tempered fellow and unable to hold a grudge for long, so by the time they reached the beach everyone was friendly again.

"Scooper, you promised me that we could all go for a trip round the bay in a motor launch," Tiger reminded him, as she stroked her pet mascot gently. "Look, there's a fine one called the *Saucy Cockle* waiting on the quayside now. Can we go in that one?"

"Alright, young Tiger, a promise is a promise," laughed Scooper, smiling down at the youngest Double Decker. "Come along, everyone, all aboard the *Saucy Cockle*."

"Come along, Albert, or we shall all be separated again," urged Billie, as she pushed him forward into the boat rather impatiently.

"I'm not too keen on sailing," said Albert, looking rather alarmed. "I think I'll stay on the sands until you get back."

He rose to his feet rather unsteadily. But just at that moment a sailor started up the engine and Albert was thrown back into his seat again.

"Too late, Albert, you'll just have to grin and bear it," laughed Spring, who was leaning over the boat catching the spray full in his face. "Besides, this is fun. I wish it would get really rough and choppy, and then it would be just smashing. Wouldn't it?" he appealed to the others, who all nodded in agreement.

All, that is, except Albert, who was slowly turning white.

"Albert, what's wrong?" cried tender-hearted little Tiger. "Don't you like sailing?"

"I'm always seasick when I'm on a boat," groaned Albert. "Oh, how I wish we were back ashore."

"Take deep breaths," advised Billie. "Poor old Albert, what a shame. Never mind, we're half way round the bay now, only the other half to go."

"And there goes Albert's breakfast," chuckled cheeky Spring, as Albert gasped and leaned over the side of the boat.

When the boat finally returned to the quay, the Double Deckers helped a still shaky Albert into a deckchair, where he recovered while they enjoyed a game of beach cricket.

"Oh, Tiger, that's another catch you've dropped!" cried Sticks crossly, as once again Tiger was hampered in catching the ball because she still held onto her toy. "Why don't you put your Tiger down on the sands?"

"What, and let someone run off with him?" retorted Tiger indignantly. "Besides, he enjoys playing cricket."

Sticks shrugged his shoulders resignedly, and bowled once again to Doughnut. The plump Double Decker gave the ball a mighty swipe and it fell with a crash onto the newspaper of a man sleeping in a deckchair.

"Gosh, I say, I *am* sorry," cried Doughnut, leaving the game to rush up and apologise.

"No harm done, old son," the little tubby man assured him with a twinkle in his eyes. "Besides, you've done me a good turn. I'm the compère of the show on the pier, and it starts in ten minutes. If you hadn't warned me I might have overslept and been late. Let's see, how many of you are there . . . take these tickets and come and see the show. I'm sure you'll enjoy it. And if any of you can perform, we have a talent competition as well. So come along and try your luck. You may win a valuable prize," he chuckled.

The Double Deckers, who were never shy of giving a display of their talents, were delighted with this idea, and they sat in the front row so that they were first on the stage when the talent competition began.

The clever comedy double act of Spring and Scooper, and the exquisite ballet dancing of Billie drew generous applause from the audience. But it was Sticks' performance on the drums, kindly lent by the show's drummer, that really had the house tapping its feet and stamping for more.

When the audience was asked to judge the competitors by the volume of applause, Sticks received a deafening ovation and was clearly the winner. He received a pass that gave him free entry to all the rides and entertainments on the nearby fairground, and the other Double Deckers received giant sticks of rock as consolation prizes.

Sticks was eager to use his free pass, and so they all went off to the fair. What a time they had!

"It's just like being up in an aeroplane," giggled Tiger, as they waited on top of the Big Wheel for the others to get into their carriages.

"I only hope we can get down again," said Billie in mock alarm, as she watched Spring, Scooper *and* Doughnut pile into the bottom carriage.

But all went well as they went round and round in giant circles, catching fascinating glimpses of all the other parts of the fairground as they circled round.

"Oh, look, there's the House of Mirrors," cried Tiger, as the sun glinted on the glass doorway to the house. "Do let's go there next."

So in they all trooped and were absolutely helpless with laughter at the sight of themselves in the contorted mirrors.

"Look how fat we look," giggled Billie to Tiger. "Almost as fat as Doughnut."

"You're even fatter at the moment," retorted Doughnut, good-naturedly. "I think I'll see if I can buy *this* mirror to take home. It makes me look so tall and thin."

"We'll try and buy one for your birthday," giggled Tiger rather nervously, as she gazed into a mirror which showed her beloved pet as a gigantic lifesize tiger. "Oh, Billie, I meant to ask you before. What did the fortune-teller say when you went to see her while we were all on the swingboats?"

"Oh, the usual things," replied Billie carelessly. "I would enjoy good health and have a long life . . . and I would soon receive an interesting letter from abroad."

"Well, that just shows what nonsense this fortune-telling lark is," scoffed Brains, whose scientific mind always wanted positive proof about anything before he believed it. "*You* don't know anyone living abroad, so how can that statement come true?"

"I have an aunt living in the States," said Spring helpfully. "Shall I ask her to write to Billie?"

"That wouldn't be the same. That's contriving to make things come true," replied Brains loftily.

Spring's face fell, and Billie squeezed his arm. "It was a nice thought anyway, Spring," she said with a grateful smile.

"Oh, let's get out of here," grumbled Albert, as he caught sight of himself in a mirror which made him look as fat as a barrel.

"Yes, I am beginning to feel a little peckish," cried Doughnut. "I think it is about time we got back to the beach for our picnic tea."

"Peckish . . . you? More like a greedy little pig," shouted Spring. "I don't know how you have the cheek to say you feel hungry," he went on. "While we were on the fairground you ate your way through three packets of popcorn, two toffee apples and a large choc ice."

"That was just a snack to keep me going until tea," grinned Doughnut.

"Tea with you is more like feeding time at the zoo," cried Sticks. "You are the nearest thing I know to a human dustman, Doughnut. You will eat anything. It must cost a small fortune to feed you."

"And it's worth every penny," remarked Doughnut smugly, as he led the party back to the beach.

Billie unpacked the hamper which they had brought with them and soon they were all munching away contentedly.

"I thought that I had put in enough food to feed an army," she remarked a little later, as she gazed at the empty hamper. "But, obviously, I was wrong. There's not one scrap of food left."

"Now, pick up all the litter and put it back in the basket," ordered Albert. "Let's leave the beach as clean and tidy as we found it. If everyone tidied up their litter my job would be much easier."

"If there was no litter to sweep up you would be out of a job," chuckled cheeky Spring. "And as for feeding an army, Billie, remember that an army marches on its stomach . . . and Doughnut's stomach is a very large one and needs a lot of filling."

"Hey, steady on, *you* were the one to eat that last squashed sardine sandwich," protested Doughnut, glaring at Spring. "Do we have to take home all those empty lemonade bottles, Billie? They will be very heavy to carry."

"Oh, surely not, to you?" cried Billie, in-

nocently. "After all, with all that food to strengthen you, you ought to be able to carry a sack of coal quite easily, never mind a picnic hamper."

Then, taking pity on Doughnut, she said with a smile, "Listen, everyone, I've just had a great idea. Let's all write a message and put it in a bottle, and throw it in the sea."

"Oh, yes, it might be washed up anywhere in the world," cried Tiger, her eyes shining with excitement.

"Probably only a few miles away on the same shore," murmured Brains, rather scornfully. But Spring noticed, with a grin, that his brainy friend was busy writing his message as he spoke.

They watched the tide take the bottles out to sea and then, very reluctantly, made their way to the station.

"Well, its been a great day," cried Scooper, as he settled himself comfortably in a corner seat. "It's a shame it's over."

But Billie, thinking of those bottles floating away on the waves, said softly to herself: "I wonder."

For the first few days after the trip to the seaside, Billie found herself looking out eagerly for the postman. But she kept her reason a secret from the rest of the Double Deckers after she had found Spring, resplendent in turban and gold earrings, 'telling fortunes' amid great laughter from the others.

"You, sir," cried Spring in ringing tones, "will one day become the doughnut-eating champion of the world," to the plump Double Decker who, as usual, was munching away at a jammy doughnut.

"And you, madam, will perform the dying duck . . . er, I mean swan," he said, turning to Billie, "before the crowned heads of Europe."

"And I see music for you, too, Sticks, possibly in the army as leader of a military band," he went on with a grin.

"I think they're all horrid," cried Billie to herself as she saw the postman in the distance. But, suddenly, she could scarcely believe her eyes, for the postman was actually waving a letter at her.

"Is this what you have been waiting for?" he asked. "It certainly looks interesting. A foreign stamp and all."

Billie tore open the envelope with trembling fingers and read the letter slowly. A happy smile spread over her face, and she read it again. Then, whistling merrily, she made her way back to the Double Deckers' den.

"I'm thinking of taking a holiday in Brittany next year," she announced casually. "My new pen pal Marcelle has invited me to stay with her."

The others stared at her in amazement.

"You mean someone actually found your letter in the bottle?" gasped Brains.

"Yes, here's her answer. She seems a great girl," replied Billie. "But of course, I knew that it was only a question of time before I received a letter from abroad. You see," she added smugly, as a parting shot, as she settled down with her writing pad, "*I* believe in fortune-tellers!"

DOUBLE DECKER FUNTIME

There once was a leader named Scooper,
Who his gang thought was simply super,
But one day in a barrel,
He decided to travel,
Now they call him 'Scooper the Cooper'.

One day a young lady named Billie,
Did something incredibly silly,
She dressed up as a flower,
And sat in a bower,
So people called her 'Daffy-down-dilly'.

A very fat boy, name of Doughnut,
Was standing in a field on one foot,
When a pain in his rear,
Made him cry out with fear:
"That old goat's just given me a butt!"

A cheery young lad called Spring,
Each day in his bath loved to sing,
But the noise that he made,
Gained no accolade,
For even the sparrows took wing!

A clever musician called Sticks,
Played just like a cat on hot bricks,
Music soft, sweet or loud,
But all who heard him avowed
It was one of his best party tricks.

Young Tiger is always so cocky,
Especially when she tries to play hockey,
She charges over the field,
And she never will yield
To opponents much bigger and more stocky!

A DELIGHT OF DANCES

Whenever the Double Deckers put on a show they always include plenty of dancing, but throughout the world there are many unusual dances, some of which have their origins far back in the mists of time.

SWIRLING SWORDS

Many dances include the use of weapons, especially swords. These dances probably originated when warlike tribes had light-hearted sport among themselves with mock battles.

One such dance is still performed regularly by the men of the small island of Bali, using their fearsome-looking kris, and walking in solemn lines, which gradually get faster until the men are running. Then a mock battle takes place, which to the awestruck onlookers appears terrifyingly realistic.

Sword dances still take place in various parts of the British Isles, especially in Scotland, where both men and women dance reels, nimbly leaping high in the air, and landing neatly in a quarter of a square made by two crossed swords placed on the ground. These dances first originated when someone invented a dance which incorporated the old Norse invaders' dances with weapons, and the gay French dances brought over the border from France by Mary Queen of Scots when she returned to her native land.

But in England the dancers hold their swords in their hands and use them to 'Kill the Fool' . . . but all in fun, of course.

They all wear colourful clothes such as white costumes piped with bright red, and gay ribbons in their hats, and often their swords are only wood, which is really essential when they use them to stab the fool.

But before they do this there is a lot of intricate swordplay to gay fiddler's music, and the dance is watched by a number of spectators, including the Doctor and Besom Betty, who are to play an important part in reviving the stricken fool.

As the fool falls, seemingly mortally wounded, the Doctor rushes to his aid with medicine and pills. But this fails to revive him, and all watch anxiously as Besom Betty arrives on the scene with her rough broom. As she sweeps the fool about with her broom, to the amusement of all he suddenly regains his health and they dance away happily together.

ANIMAL MASQUERADE

Some dances involve the dancers in a masquerade in which they don animal disguises and act just like these creatures.

In Africa, before a hunt, a member of a native tribe will dress up as a lion, a deer or whatever other animal is being hunted, and the others will dance about and pretend to kill him, and so ensure a successful hunt.

The Balinese also have a story dance called a *ketjak,* in which men dress up as monkeys and act exactly like these mischievous creatures as they dance out the story of the revenge a god takes upon these naughty animals when they kill his favourite servant.

In parts of northern Russia the people perform dances in which the dancers pretend to be reindeers and seals, and in another dance they recall the days when their ancestors paid homage to the mighty eagle, by dancing round a dagger in a way which symbolises the manner in which the eagle hunted for its food.

SLAPS AND SPRINGS

Several countries have dances which include lots of jumping about and the slapping of hands and legs.

In France they have a dance called 'Planting Cabbages' in which they hop or walk round in a circle, constantly changing direction and stamping their feet on every sixteenth step they take, symbolising the time when they planted cabbages firmly in the ground by stamping on them.

A similar dance is well-known in Holland as the 'Seven Jumps'. Men, dressed in the traditional baggy trousers, striped shirts and astrakhan caps, and women in black aprons over multi-coloured skirts topped with richly embroidered blouses and wide-winged caps, sing a song as they dance, jumping high at the end of each verse and performing a different mime at the same time. The seventh and last jump is the most spectacular of all, for the performers turn head over heels after falling flat on the ground and touching their foreheads.

For special celebrations in Austrian villages people dance the lively *schuhplattler,* in which the dancers slap shoes, shorts, knees and thighs as part of the dance, and indulge in friendly, light-hearted rivalry to see who can jump or somersault the highest in the air. They also pretend to slap each other's faces hard; but this is only in fun and the result of very clever miming.

A SPECTACULAR MAYPOLE DANCE

Most people have seen a traditional maypole dance on May morning, when graceful dancers weave in and out and round about a gaily decorated flowered pole, twisting and turning their coloured ribbons as they dance.

But in remote villages a short distance from Mexico City, a different maypole dance takes place, not on the ground, but many feet up in the air, and the dancers or flyers, or *voladores* as they are known, are suspended from their waists by stout ropes to the tall maypole.

But before the dance begins, each flyer stands on a framework at the top of the maypole and plays a musical instrument and when, at a signal from their leader, each man begins to swing or 'fly' upside-down round the maypole, he still plays his flute or drum!

The dance recalls the days of Cortez when the Indians believed that four great birds were responsible for guarding the four points of the compass, and homage was paid to these birds in a dance to keep men safe.

Today six men fly, instead of the four birds, five wearing red breeches, white shirts and gaily coloured hats, and one wearing a skirt is said to represent a brave Indian girl who helped and befriended the great Cortez.

Often there are accidents during this dance, but it still continues, and as the ropes slowly lower these brave men to the ground, they thoroughly deserve the applause which greets them for performing the most spectacular maypole dance ever seen.

Billie's bus quiz

All the Double Deckers are interested in buses, especially Billie, who has set this quiz to see if you know as much as she does! If you can answer each of these questions correctly, you will be sure of a big welcome in the Double Deckers' Den.

1. In which city would you travel by *motoscafi?* venice.

2. What was the name of the first man to introduce the first horse-drawn public transport vehicle in Paris in 1662? Blaise Pascal.

3. What else do Swiss buses carry besides passengers and luggage? Mail

4. What year did George Shillibear start operating a regular horsebus service in London? 1829.

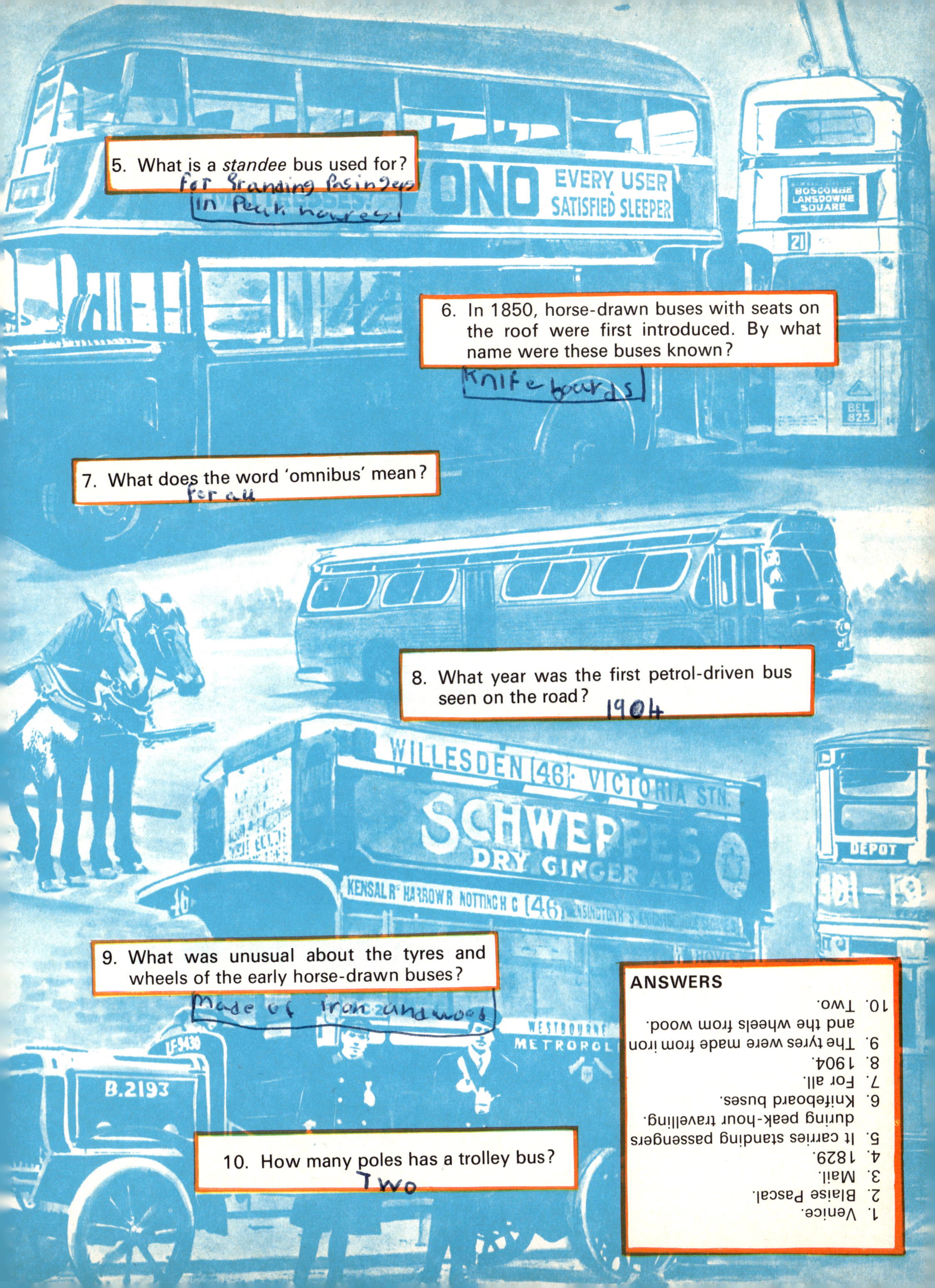

5. What is a *standee* bus used for?

For standing pasingers in Peak houres

6. In 1850, horse-drawn buses with seats on the roof were first introduced. By what name were these buses known?

knife boards

7. What does the word 'omnibus' mean?

for all

8. What year was the first petrol-driven bus seen on the road?

1904

9. What was unusual about the tyres and wheels of the early horse-drawn buses?

Made of iron and wood

10. How many poles has a trolley bus?

Two

ANSWERS

1. Venice.
2. Blaise Pascal.
3. Mail.
4. 1829.
5. It carries standing passengers during peak-hour travelling.
6. Knifeboard buses.
7. For all.
8. 1904.
9. The tyres were made from iron and the wheels from wood.
10. Two.

Brain teasers

Brains Come on, Doughnut, put that knickerbocker glory down and see if you can answer this: which is the right side of a cake?

Doughnut Well, it's bound to be the side that's eaten, because the other side is left!

Brains is quite convinced that his brain power is far superior to that of the other Double Deckers, and so he has decided to prove this with the use of his infallible teasers. Or infallible, so he thinks! However, the gang aren't so easily taken in. Especially when Tiger is peeping, ready to help with any answers that they might not get!

Brains I'll bet you can't answer this one, Sticks. What are the largest ants in the whole world?

Sticks Giants . . . . . thought you'd caught me that time, didn't you? *(In fact, if it hadn't been for Tiger, Sticks might well have been caught out!)*

Brains What about you, Billie? Can you tell me which is the most valuable letter in the alphabet?

Billie Where did you get that out of—the ark? The letter C, naturally, because it can turn *ash* into *cash*.

Brains Can you tell me what may lose, but never ever wins, Scooper?

Scooper Huh! Kids' stuff! A clock, of course.

Brains Hey, Spring! What's worse than raining cats and dogs?

Spring How about *hailing taxis,* Brains?

Brains You're my last hope, Tiger. Why did the jam roll?

Tiger Hmm, that's easy, even for me! Because it saw the kitchen sink!

TIGER AT THE ZOO

"Hello, young Tiger, I'm glad that I bumped into you this morning," said Scooper, as he smiled warmly at the youngest Double Decker whom he had just met in the High Street. "I have something rather special I want to ask you."

"Are you cross with me, Scooper?" asked the little girl anxiously. "I didn't really mean to hit you quite so hard with my tiger yesterday. Honestly, I didn't!"

"Oh, forget it," grinned Scooper reassuringly. "No, what I wanted to ask you was where you would like to go on your birthday? We would all like to give you a special treat, and Billie says you must choose what we shall do. Pick anywhere you like, the treat's on us."

"Oh, what a lovely idea!" cried Tiger. "Thank you all very much." She thought hard for a moment, and then she said eagerly: "Could we go to the zoo? I have always wanted to show my tiger what a real tiger looks like."

"Right, the zoo it shall be," said Scooper kindly. "I'll tell the others, and we'll meet at the den early on Saturday morning so that we can have a full day."

For once, everyone arrived promptly at the den, and the Double Deckers were the first people in the zoo that morning.

"Now, where do you want to go first?" asked Billie. "To see the tigers, I suppose?" she asked with a chuckle.

"No, let's keep the best bit until the last," replied Tiger, hugging her pet mascot hard in her excitement. "Let's go and see the elephants."

"Doughnut's relatives, you mean," laughed Sticks, easily dodging a blow from his chubby friend with the skill of long practice. "I believe that we can have a ride on one elephant's back. Would you like that, Tiger?"

"Yes, if you'll all come too," insisted Tiger, looking rather nervous at the idea. "I hope we won't all fall off."

"Oh, we shall sit in a kind of seat called a howdah," explained Brains, eager to air his

knowledge as usual. "It will be quite an experience for us all."

But it was an experience that Doughnut was not destined to share, for when the keeper saw him he waved Doughnut away indignantly. "You're not sitting on Rani," he shouted. "There's such a thing as cruelty to animals, you know. Rani would collapse with your weight on top of her."

"Nonsense, Doughnut only looks large," insisted Tiger. "He weighs as light as a feather."

"Yes, a feather bed," murmured Sticks to Scooper. "I shouldn't worry too much about Doughnut," he said to Tiger, as she searched for him amongst the crowds from her seat on Rani's back. "He'll be quite content to wait for us by that sweet stall until we return."

"Yes, I can see his mouth bulging with toffee from here," smiled Billie. "I *am* enjoying this ride. What shall we see next?"

"How about going to watch the chimpanzees' tea party?" suggested Spring. "That should be great fun!"

The others eagerly approved of this suggestion, and soon they were all laughing as one chimpanzee poured tea into dainty cups while the others ate cakes, happily chattering together.

"Those cakes look good," murmured Doughnut, as he gazed longingly at the laden table.

The chimpanzee must have heard him, for suddenly it rose from the table, picked up a plate of cakes and walked over and offered one to Doughnut.

"Why, thank you very much, I don't mind if I do," laughed the fat Double Decker as he nimbly selected the biggest and creamiest cake from the plate. "What hospitable folk you zoo animals are."

"I thought *we* were supposed to feed the *animals* titbits," said Spring as he steered Doughnut away firmly in the direction of the bird house. "And don't go stealing any seed, Doughnut. Remember *that* is strictly for the birds."

"Oh, I don't know," teased Scooper. "Perhaps a little seed might improve his singing voice. It's pretty horrible at the moment. Even the cats run away when Doughnut starts to sing."

"Haha, very funny," retorted Doughnut. "I haven't noticed *you* being flooded with offers to sing on TV . . . or did I miss your recent TV spectacular?"

"Oh, they did ask him to take part—to sweep the stage afterwards," laughed Sticks, who had recently won a junior talent competition playing the drums, and so felt quite safe to joke about Scooper.

As they entered the bird house, Scooper gave Sticks a playful push, but unfortunately he pushed rather harder than he intended and Sticks went sprawling on the floor.

"Oh, sorry, Sticks, let me help you up," said Scooper, feeling rather ashamed of himself.

"Yes, five, six, pick up sticks," croaked a voice.

It was a brightly-coloured parrot that spoke, regarding the Double Deckers with its sharp, beady eyes. Its remark caused them all to burst out laughing, and Tiger sighed with relief as she watched Sticks and Scooper set off to tour the exhibits together, their quarrel quite forgotten.

"You would never believe that birds could sound so much like people, would you?" said Billie to Tiger, as they listened to the loud noise all the birds made.

"No, and they show off just like people too," said Tiger, as she watched a beautiful peacock display its magnificent tail. "Let's go somewhere quieter now, please, Scooper. My head is beginning to ache with all this noise."

"We'll go and have a picnic lunch now, and afterwards we'll go to see the sealions," said Scooper kindly. "Come along, everyone. We'll buy some food from the shop over there, and then find a pleasant spot for our picnic."

Soon they were all munching away happily on the grass beneath a shady tree in part of the zoo's refreshment area. Scooper and the boys had bought lots of food, including sandwiches, pies, cakes and biscuits and several bottles of lemonade.

"Goodness, we shall never eat all that!" Billie had gasped as they had arrived at the picnic spot laden with food.

But, of course, she had forgotten Doughnut's

gigantic appetite and, sure enough, long after all the others had finished, Doughnut was still eating steadily.

"I really enjoyed that," he said, patting his stomach contentedly as they carefully cleared up the litter. "You know, I think I wouldn't mind being an animal in this zoo. A comfortable home and plenty to eat. What more can one ask for?"

"Plenty, but what you are going to get is a little exercise to walk off that mound of food," cried Spring, pulling a reluctant Doughnut to his feet. "Come along, gang, we shall have to hurry if we want to see the sealion show. It starts in five minutes and it is right at the other side of the zoo."

The others got hurriedly to their feet and were just in time to get a good view of the sealions' pool as their trainer came out to start the show.

"Aren't they clever?" gasped Tiger, as she watched the sealions juggle with coloured balls and throw them to each other, catching them nimbly each time between their flippers. "They certainly deserve the fish their keeper is giving them."

"*They* obviously think so too," laughed Sticks. "Look how they are applauding themselves by clapping their flippers together. Self-praise is no recommendation, you know, old chaps," he chuckled.

"You should know," retorted Billie, who had been very impressed by the sealions' act. "You are always blowing your own trumpet, or should I say your drums?"

"Goodness, this show has lasted a long time," cried Sticks, who did not like the turn the conversation was taking. "I think we had better go and see the tigers now, young Tiger. Then it will be time to catch the bus home."

Scooper and Billie exchanged an amused smile with Brains and Spring as they all realised that Sticks had craftily changed the conversation. But little Tiger was too happy talking about the animals she was going to see to notice.

"Aren't they wonderful creatures, pet?" she cried as she held up her little mascot so that he would get a closer look at the regal animals stalking behind their iron bars. "How fierce and proud they look!"

"Hey, kiddy, hold that pose a minute!" called a voice. The others turned in surprise, and were just in time to see young Mike, a reporter from the local paper, taking a picture of Tiger.

"This may be just what I need to impress my Editor," cried Mike. "Our chief photographer is leaving, and I'd like the job, if I can get it. Don't forget to look in the rag tomorrow, Tiger, and if I get the job, I'll buy you the biggest box of chocolates you have ever seen in your life."

"Goody, now I still have something to look forward to," cried Tiger happily as they made their way over to the exit at the zoo. "Thank you all very much for my birthday treat. I have enjoyed every minute of the day."

"We're very glad," said Billie, putting her arm around the youngest Double Decker. "Now, let's all make sure that we buy a copy of the paper tomorrow to see your photograph."

When Tiger arrived at the den the next day she was greeted with loud cries of delight.

"Did you see your photograph?" cried Spring. "Look, here it is on the front page and the caption says *Tiger amongst the tigers!* It's the best picture of the week."

"Hasn't my tiger come out well?" cried the little girl happily. "And look, everyone, what Mike has given me. Do take as many chocolates as you like. There must be hundreds in this box. It weighs four pounds and has such a pretty picture on the front. I shall be able to keep my handkerchiefs in it when it is empty."

"Then let's start emptying it straight away," said Doughnut cheekily, as he selected a chocolate from the box which Tiger held out to him. "Now, I wonder," he added thoughtfully as he munched away happily, "I wonder if Mike would like a picture of me in the cake shop? *Doughnut amongst the Doughnuts,*" he explained to the others. "And, of course, in order that the picture has the authentic touch, I should have to be sampling a doughnut."

"Trust Doughnut to think of an idea in which he could indulge in his favourite hobby," laughed Scooper, as he cut out Tiger's picture and pinned it up on the wall. "Look, everyone, now we've really got a pin-up of our very own."

"Two pin-ups, you mean," replied Tiger firmly, although she was blushing shyly. "Me *and* my tiger!"

for
Goodbye